Matching Services to Markets

Matching Services to Markets

The Role of the Human Sensorium in Shaping Service-Intensive Markets

H.B. Casanova

BEP BUSINESS EXPERT PRESS

Matching Services to Markets: The Role of the Human Sensorium in Shaping Service-Intensive Markets

Copyright © Business Expert Press, LLC, 2016.

First published in 2016 by
Business Expert Press, LLC
222 East 46th Street, New York, NY 10017
www.businessexpertpress.com

ISBN-13: 978-1-63157-307-1 (paperback)
ISBN-13: 978-1-63157-308-8 (e-book)

Business Expert Press Service Systems and Innovations in Business and Society Collection

Collection ISSN: 2326-2664 (print)
Collection ISSN: 2326-2699 (electronic)

Cover and interior design by Exeter Premedia Services Private Ltd., Chennai, India

First edition: 2016

10 9 8 7 6 5 4 3 2 1

Printed in the United States of America.

"Wee felt it before in fenfe;
but now we know it by fcience;

wee found it before in operation,
but now wee fee it in fpeculation"

EDWARD MISSELDEN
ENGLISH ADVOCATE FOR MERCANTILISM
1623

Abstract

Every creature builds its niche in engagement with its environment. Such engagements, repeated over time, invariably result in stable exchanges supporting a particular species.

Every species maintains its exchanges using its unique *sensorium*, its own aggregated set of sensory channels it uses to see and frame the world around it.

Our sensorium dictates the unique way we discover our worlds. It determines the reach, the range, the limits, the apprehended spectra, the blind spots, and the sutures among the sensory channels by which we gain *inbound* impressions of our wider environs.

As well, our sensorium conditions how we think, judge, and how we launch *outbound* action, as we build our very human exchanges into societies.

It engraves and projects itself on both the learnings and initiatives we deploy to impose meaning and intent onto our wider human world. It determines our structures, our processes and the materiel we use to build out our socially networked exchanges. In the economic realm, these exchanges, structured uniquely by our very human sensorium, become formalized as Markets.

Understanding our sensorium, seeing its projective power, its emergent properties, and its corresponding fault lines and tectonic zones as it governs and even dictates our social structures, can greatly clarify our understanding of market architecture itself: structure, process, and materiel.

With these deep landmarks mapped out, we can catalyze great progress in further consolidating a robust Science of Service and Service Innovation. Spurring that on is the dominant intent and exploration of this book.

Keywords

Abram Maslow, Binaural Hearing, Breakthrough, Commodity, CONTROL, Couplets of Elemental Value, DELIVERY, Efficiency, Foveal Vision, Institutional imperatives, Intent-Driven "Cockpit," Parafovea (Parafoveal Belt), Peripheral Vision, Planning, Punctuated Spectrum, Sensorium, STRATEGY, Value Co-Creation

Contents

Foreword

What you have in your hand is far from the typical business book. This book does not promote a particular point of view as a take-it-or-leave-it prescription. It is not an advocacy of the latest nostrum, but rather a guide to the canonical issues that arise in seemingly novel garb at each twist and turn of the cycles of innovation and market maturity. Butch Casanova invites you to explore a rich tapestry of possibilities, within a timeless framework of business and personal development. He has created a navigation device, pointing out fascinating landmarks, and opening up views into inviting spaces you'll want to further explore.

As a contribution to service system innovation for business and society, this slim volume draws on Butch's wealth of experience at the interface between technology and business, as well as years of deep study. As a student of James Grier Miller's work on living systems, his viewpoint is permeated with the understanding of businesses as transindividual life-forms sensing and acting in the environment of exchange of services and materiel.

Butch makes two key points that apply to the past, present, and future of enterprise. He calls our attention to five absolute managerial imperatives that exist in every business: the key domains of Strategy, Control, and Delivery, along with two interfacing zones of Planning and Efficiency. These five imperatives help organize our thoughts about the roles, personalities, and mindsets required for business success. He then intersects the five imperatives with a spectrum of value creation that has "*commodities* on one end and *breakthroughs* on the other. Between those two pillars lie every market opportunity humans may encounter."

Within the context of his imperative and offering matrix, Butch takes us on a vivid roller-coaster ride through a panorama of science, industry, and economics, as well as history, literature, and popular culture. He uses scenarios from bull riding and casino gambling, to energy-futures strategy of Southwest Airlines, and from the Mongol hordes to MCI and McDonald's. Along the way the reader is rewarded by exposure to his elegant, even courtly, prose, featuring such gems as "signal flares flashing which of the imperatives may be in play at different levels of managerial concern," "today's algorithm of success has in it tomorrow's obsolescence and decline," and "the bias toward fearsome atmospherics in those suites is legendary."

What I am about to say should probably come with a spoiler alert, because it signals that much of the book is a handbook for pattern matching, rather than a linear narrative. The following statement clarifies much of the intent, and the value, of this volume: "This analysis becomes a sieve, sifting out what a service/materiel combination must contain, to meet the objectives of the client, once his/her objectives have been properly parsed out." This book provides a toolkit for you, the reader, to analyze a business, a career, or an opportunity, whether for yourself or acting in the role of adviser, coach, or consultant.

Butch's depth and breadth of knowledge is phenomenal, and I am personally grateful that he has committed this sampler of his thinking to writing. I'll be referring to it often, and now it is available to you, as well!

Doug McDavid, February 2016

Acknowledgments

This work and its contemplated companion volumes would have remained figments of a labored imagination had these patrons not lent their support to the work of creating them:

My sweet Australian wife tops the list, for her patient support, her willingness to suspend disbelief—and for her heroic forbearance;

My resilient friend and companion-in-ink, Doug McDavid, rates a grand salute for his ready willingness to read, comment, and debate at all hours of the day;

Jim Spohrer, singly among a 38-year parade of corporate colleagues, saw in the proposed work insights of value; he stands as its most authoritative sponsor.

Author's Prefatory Notes

The Origins of This Investigation into the Human Sensorium

The roots of this exploration of our sensorium began for the author as early as 1960, when the functional disparity between macular vision and peripheral vision in humans became an object of curiosity. The curiosity intensified, comparing our human visual system to those found in other species, as in the case of, for example, dragonflies, with their visual apparatus providing panoramas approaching 360° in extent.

Such disparities naturally drove curiosity about the disparate world-views such sensory systems would present to each of the two species: *Homo sapiens* and *Anax junius*, the common Green Darner dragonfly.

On the one hand, we, humans, omnivorous tool builders with a general-purpose biped body plan, live out lives embedded in social networks; on the other, we have in dragon flies, elegantly equipped fighter pilots, evolved to scan all around themselves, and easily able to fly up, down, forward, and backward. In short, they are equipped with a sensorium brilliantly organized to support lightning predation of amphibians, fish, insects, and crustaceans.

That early curiosity about the sensoria and worldviews specific to different species emerged again, once the author became embedded in the world of business, an archetypal human societal network.

It became increasingly obvious with continuing experience in business and market operations that the architecture of our uniquely human sensorium, with its strengths and weaknesses, had suffused itself throughout the processes, systems, provisioning, and structures of our enterprises, our markets, and our institutions. It underlays them all: We build as we see, as we hear, as we feel, as we touch.[1]

It became clear as well, that it creates surprising congruencies in vertical structure across the boundaries of even competing enterprises; further, identical institutional roles are quite common even laterally, across enterprises and industries, with these roles differentiating their incumbents almost as distinctly as speciation would do:

> "A CFO is still a green eye shade, regardless." "You production guys are all the same," "Show me a CEO who, under that tailored suit, isn't a scary, amped-up gambler, and I'll show you a loser!" "The first thing we do, let's kill all the lawyers."[2]

These insights originated in intuitions on the commanding role our complementary visual systems play over our societal structures, but they grew to envelop all the conscious sensory channels (hearing, touch, and so on) serving intentional activity.[3]

Moreover, it was evident that other players will have similarly seen their insights emerge and elaborate over time, starting from a primitive intuition and developing out into more general working theories amenable to testing and validation.

Thus, the leitmotif of this book, and its homage to Edward Misselden, by profession a 17th-century trader most often engaged with

---

[1] This ongoing elaboration of an early intuition was particularly illuminated over time by the world painted for us by two disparate thinkers, James Grier Miller, the preeminent architect of Living Systems Theory: Miller, J.G. 1978. *Living Systems*. (New York: McGraw-Hill). Print; and by Fernand Braudel, in his three magisterial-volumes on the interpenetrating rise of civilization and capitalism: Braudel, F. 1982. *Civilization and Capitalism, 15th–18th Century*. Volumes I–III. (New York: Harper & Row). Print. The latter stages of the development of our intuitions were guided by the contributions of James Spohrer, as in his work: Spohrer, J.C., and L.E. Freund. 2013. *Advances in the Human Side of Service Engineering*. (Boca Raton, FL: Taylor & Francis). Print.

[2] Shakespeare, W. *Henry VI*, Part II, Act IV, Scene II, Line 73. (A perennial crowd pleaser).

[3] As opposed to the subliminal, somatic senses serving autonomic processes.

the East India Company, and in the disputatious climate of the day, a theorist and partisan pamphleteer for early Mercantilism. He remains compelling to us today for the Baconian thought processes he threaded through, which turn out to be perennials for other thinkers who begin with a small mental itch that becomes a raging fever until it is brought under the sway of a systematic, testable theory, useful to theoreticians and practitioners alike.

Misselden is memorable in that he first fell upon and ferreted out the lineaments of the phenomenon economists know of today as the Balance of Trade. In his most comprehensive work, on his page 130,[4] we find his lapidary couplets:

Wee felt it before in sense, but now we know it by science;

Wee found it before in operation; but now wee see it in speculation.[5]

That in a nutshell forms the impetus for this work: To take the primary intuitions we have—in this case regarding our **sensorium**—and to lay bare in a systematic way their larger impact on the world we've inherited, and which we as regents must recreate for later generations.

This is particularly relevant to our discussions of for-value offerings as they evolve from inert products to quicksilver service transactions amenable to a scientific analysis.

As we confront the grand march of intention and embedded intelligence in market operations, each step requires that we will have "felt it before in sense," and work until "we know it by science."

This evolution has gathered force and rigor as it proceeded, as in such examples as these:

---

[4] Misselden, E. (1623) 1971. *The Circle of Commerce: Or the Balance of Trade*, 130. (New York: A. M. Kelley).

[5] *"Science"* in 17th-century usage roughly equated to our 21st-century "conscious, organized knowledge," and *"speculation"* anticipated our "scientific investigation." A note about Misselden's "wee": Orthography in the 17th-century was still a sandlot game with rules made up as one went along.

- From the oral and hand-scribbled recipe notes accompanying grandma's buttermilk drop biscuits;
- Through the drivers' handbooks distributed with early automobiles;
- To the embedded plugboard logic in early looms and later electronic accounting machines;
- To the explosion of reactive and anticipatory software dominating the computer revolution; and, most recently,
- Arriving at Service Science: Melding under real-time control, the complementary intentions of buyer and seller in the emergent realm of cocreation in service offering design and planning.

Let us proceed now to retrace for ourselves this evolution as it unfolds in the world of market operations.

Situating This Book in a Larger Architecture of Markets

The triple helix of the human sensorium,[6] with its major strands: intellect, judgment, and volition, is a kind of grand armature upon which all human social endeavor is splined and interwoven; it constitutes for us a deeply shrouded, but profoundly controlling architecture underpinning all human social endeavor. Its strongest external manifestations are the tripartite, interwoven elements of structure, process, and materiel.

Making explicit the sinews of this triply stranded framework is a premier intent of this exploration. In this introductory work, we address the *time-invariant* **structures** of exchanges and markets. These structures include tripartite hierarchies of executive control (production, finance, strategy), the corresponding zones of influence they call into play (delivery, control, vision), and the limitations on initiative these zones of control impose on the players in each distinct zone, for example,

---

[6] The parts of the brain or the mind concerned with the reception and interpretation of sensory stimuli; broadly: the entire sensory apparatus *Merriam-Webster*. *Merriam-Webster*. n.d. Web. January 24, 2016.

- "You bean-counters don't understand the kluge we manage down here in production";
- "The glad-handing suits in GHQ just gloss over our problems in sourcing new investment";
- "Even as CEO, I have the devil of a time driving the team to buy into my market vision."

Such invariant structures represent but one vector of the three which our sensorium evolves when it begins to frame our wider human world; the succeeding two are the *temporal* **processes** the structures support, and the *flows of* **materiel** coursing through those processes, all to create societal change.

When we have completed this introduction to:

- *Time-Invariant Structures* the sensorium creates in markets;

We will treat in Volume II:

- *Temporal Processes* that the sensorium engenders within markets. (For example, the punctuated evolution of breakthrough ideas along a standard natural history to market success and final commodity obsolescence.);

And finally, Volume III will address:

- *Materiel Flows* drawn or provisioned through markets in channels conditioned by the same sensorium. (For example, feedstocks of petroleum crude pumped through refineries; funds being drawn down from lines of credit to replenish inventory levels, canvassing of Expressions of Intent found on Twitter, to gauge consumer interest in selecting brand alternatives.)

We proceed now to give ourselves over to the power of the human sensorium, and make its architecture work for us in the world of markets and exchanges.

CHAPTER 1

Mapping a Course into Markets

Dragons Indeed

Early modern European navigators and captains put ships and men out onto intercontinental expanses that were for them largely a separate planet. They pushed off into oceans armed only with early compasses, closely-held logbooks, and portolan charts of soundings and headings gleaned from perhaps 3,500 years of riverine and littoral punting, these punctuated only by chancy passages in single-masted galleys and cogs across inland waters like the Mediterranean, the Baltic, or the Black Sea.

In thrall to flawed Ptolemaic geography and astronomy, they puzzled at every new turn, trying to conform to this received, erroneous tradition, the conflicting facts they found.

Men like Columbus and Hudson, Da Gama, and Magellan, placing better bets on innovative three-masted caravels and carracks, still labored along in only the first five or so feet of surface draft. They had few hints of the structures, processes, or materiel making up the deep expanses sweeping under their keels: continental shelves, abyssal plains, layered pelagic zones of increasing depth and pressure, trenches yawning open as far as 36,000 feet below them, midocean ridges, uncharted reefs, and shoals.

Barely acquainted with the huge climatic "rivers" overhead (the Trades, the Easterlies, and Westerlies) against which their ships were beating, they had only glancing awareness that these systems spin saltwater circuits moored in the great intercontinental basins, and that these in turn drive vast oceanic currents[1] that ease or impede a sailor's course.

---

[1] North Atlantic: the Gulf Stream; North Pacific: the Kuroshio Current; South Atlantic: the Brazil Current; South Pacific: the East Australian Current; and Indian Ocean: the Agulhas Current.

If these were not hurdles enough, they paid out in lives for their ignorance of human limits looming ahead from extended shipboard confinement, exposure, and inadequate diet. Lethal scurvy, dysentery, malaria, typhus, syphilis, and the ship's surgeon's gift of gangrene were just a few of the possible prices paid on any passage of more than a month. Only decades of shared experience and admiralty study operated to bring all these unknowns under even halting control. Thus the spirit, if not the letter of "There be dragons" characterized the age.[2]

It is no accident that even now, our confusion over some impasse can evoke the timeless response, "I'm all at sea about that."

It's a Jungle Out There

To those of us navigating amid a marketplace, this confusion is familiar. Academic treatments of market structure and dynamics may add substantially to understanding.[3] Even shared watercooler lore itself can help to a point.

But professionals working to drive change know that markets are arenas of sudden surprise and upset. How many of us have scanned across a turnout of decision makers and their staffs, our lines rehearsed, our answers to potential objections at our fingertips, and our career-making PowerPoint slides resequenced as recently as 4:30 a.m. of the day at hand?

How many of us have looked across the faces, picking out the sponsor for our project, and the C-level executives who must give the nod to our

---

[2] "Hic sunt dracones" In Meyer, R. 2013. "No Old Maps Actually Say 'Here Be Dragons.'" *The Atlantic,* December 12, www.theatlantic.com/technology/archive/2013/12/no-old-maps-actually-say-here-be-dragons/282267/ (accessed April 04, 2015).

[3] The traditional gold standard for many of us in this, has been Philip Kotler's body of work: Kotler, P., and K.L. Keller. 2011. *Marketing Management.* 14th ed. (Harlow: Pearson Education).

propositions? Have we not launched our pitch, to find critical members of the staff squinting at their phones, while the C-level people attend to the murmurs of urgent assistants? Haven't we noted that the questions posed by our audiences often seem to be off-topic, and wildly incongruent with their titles: Finance execs musing over fleet truck routing, and CTOs asking about possible brand extensions into discount malls, a CEO asking if we can cut to the chase before he has to hit an awaiting limo downstairs?

What we've all feared most at the proposal stage of projects is the old threat of the "mouse getting loose in the room," where two or more ranking executives pounce upon a lively side issue to chase around the table, entirely extraneous to the topic you need decided, while the clock runs out on your allotted time.

If you run your proposals through these gauntlets without major scars, the implementation process can be equally daunting, with change requests and market shifts causing tactical adjustments that may be driven by legitimate requirements—or from political moves by players completely unmindful of consequences they are unleashing.

Mismatches between titles and executive interests, distractions posed by competing obligations, and pet vocabularies, simple idle curiosity shunting meetings into side spurs—these are all stumbling blocks in executive decision making that churn decisions about implementing change in market operations.

At the daily operational level, the granular experience of customer demands that overtake one's best efforts at day or timer planning, the arrival of unanticipated personnel upsets, the serving of legal challenges by competitors and regulators, and the general din of day-to-day workspace interaction, is all reminiscent of the hourly challenges faced by our maritime forebears facing the latest squall and freshet hitting their ships abeam. It can easily drive the best of plans into an aimless scrum.

The yearly publication of myriad titles on markets and marketing, promising indispensable stratagems to break through this continuing churn, betrays the need for deeper answers on how to navigate both the grand expanses and the abyssal deeps[4] of markets, whether one is selling or buying, whether dealing materiel or services.[5]

Where then to find primary insights with real stopping power that soak to the bone? How to chart and negotiate markets with a taproot grasp truly congruent to their looming, formidable features of structure, process, and materiel flow?

---

[4] This biaxial challenge is often portrayed succinctly as the effort to develop a "T-shaped perspective" on markets, where the vertical is the province of the ensiled component, product, or sector specialist, and the horizontal is the world of the empathetic, strategic communicator Cf. T-Shaped Professionals. *The Service Thinking Framework*. CVC Group, n.d. Web.

[5] Throughout this book, *Goods* and *Materiel* always equate to *Operand Resources*; and *Services* equate to *Operant Resources* after Constantin and Lusch: for conceptual clarity, as well, we use the term *Product* sparingly, because it may also too easily reinforce the vernacular sense of offerings as exclusively inert "stuff," shorn of the catalyzing impetus of *Service*—their reason for being. Cf. Constantin, J.A., and R.F. Lusch. 1994. *Understanding Resource Management: How to Deploy Your People, Products, and Processes for Maximum Productivity*. (Oxford, OH: Planning Forum). Cf. Vargo, S.L., and R.F. Lusch. 2004. "Evolving to a New Dominant Logic for Marketing." *Journal of Marketing* 68, no. 1, pp. 1–17. Web.

CHAPTER 2

And the Answer Is—Exchanges

Driven by the inescapable basics of our biology, and acknowledging the growing insights offered by sociobiology, this book builds on the basic insight that critical to understanding any market in question, is a deeper understanding of the underlying basics of **exchanges**. These are the indispensable engines driving all transactions of value to living beings. It is no happenstance that a perennial synonym for "markets" is "exchanges."

Exchanges are at base, structured arenas wherein process flows of information, energy, and materiel, upon regular repetition, engrain stable complexity, of ordered process, and architecture into an otherwise entropic domain. They locally, and for the lifetime of the living system modulating them, prevent the local flow of entropy from draining it out into an inert ground state.[1]

They are the catalyzing engines separating an iron ingot's irreversible oxidization into a mass of rust, from a Giant Sequoia[2] photosynthesizing multiple environmental resources to span itself across many hundreds of years of life.

Exchanges understood as such originate from living or even viruses: "near-living" creatures. Every species of living being survives by:

- Clearing out a defensible space around it (its arena, or in the instance of burrowing species, its *precinct*);

---

[1] A corollary is that the stability imposed on that domain decreases the possibilities inherent in the domain. The domain becomes an abstracted, structured subset of the larger environment, with aspects of intent governing its abstracted structure.

[2] *Sequoiadendron giganteum.*

- Activating filter membranes at the periphery of its domain that repel dangerous elements of its environment, and draw in elements useful to its survival through various methods;[3]
- Evolving feedback mechanisms to modulate the activities of these filters; and
- Optimizing its surrounds by its own movement, or the shaping of the surrounds themselves.

More-evolved species may control multitudes of exchanges, involving all manner of materiel, energy, and information resources.

In every case, the filtering in these exchanges is driven by its *sensorium*,[4] the repertoire of sensory channels available to the species in question. The sensorium, uniquely specific to each species, underpins for it a unique perception of the surrounding world, and interacts intimately with whatever levels of intelligence the species has, to help keep it in existence.

---

[3] Active uptake pathways; Diffusion; Osmosis; Transpiration; Digestion; Absorption, and so on.

[4] *Merriam-Webster.* www.merriam-webster.com/dictionary/sensorium (accessed July 20, 2015), "*Sensorium*: the parts of the brain or the mind concerned with the reception and interpretation of sensory stimuli; *broadly*: the entire sensory apparatus."

CHAPTER 3

Markets

Exchanges Unique to *Homo sapiens*

Our own evolved human sensorium provides us with all the basic inputs we have about the world around us. Our sizable aggregation of sensory channels has been slowly amalgamated from disparate evolutionary resources beginning as early as 1.5 billion years ago. This sensorial toolset has channels of considerable power (e.g., sight) over our overt *sentient* activity, as well as channels that operate quite far below the threshold of our consciousness,[1] those serving the autonomic nervous system.

Our sensorium also creates the *illusion* that we enjoy a smooth, uninterrupted panorama of our world, giving us uninterrupted data about phenomena as small as individual ants in their nests, and reaching out to the grandeurs of our Milky Way.

In actuality, this panorama does have discontinuities and blind spots,[2] and it does involve pauses and hitches in our perception of the world around us, as one channel hands off to another, the perceptual task at hand.

All of them, taken as a bundle, are more like gears in a vehicle transmission, requiring changes, shifts, and even lurches among them, to keep momentum underway, felt even when the transmissions are automatic. These shifts and modulations point to the fact that these differing resources have moved into play within our physiognomy as a punctuated

---

[1] For example, Protopathic and epicritic sensibilities, exteroception, interoception, and proprioception among others. Cf. Nolte, J. 2002. *The Human Brain*. 5th ed. (MO: Mosley).

[2] As instances: the *scotoma*, the outright blind spot, as in vertebrate eyes like ours, and the less richly populated sensors of the parafoveal band; as well as orientation deafness when identical sounds arrive at opposite sides of the head.

aggregation of discrete physical structures (fovea, tympani, and so on), interpolated by the "wetware" of innervated tissue. This does not add up to a smooth continuum; it constitutes rather, an aggregation with blending interpolations.

> There is a rich body of knowledge regarding the evolution of *sensoria*, varying widely by the species in question; for a much fuller exploration of the *sensorium* unique to our own species, Homo sapiens, please refer to our Appendix B: The Roots of Market Structure in Biology and Sociobiology.

Each channel handoff depends on surrounding interpolative logic to create the perception of smooth transitions. Whether it is the saccadic eye movements jittering along to support sight, or our head movements, nodding and turning to augment the precision of our hearing, our senses are in constant vibration and interaction to cobble together for us the panoramic apperception we need to cope with our surroundings.

The larger gaps where physical structure is bridged by learned, interpolating logic actually **cleave fissures** into our vision of the world around us; these delimit privileged and subordinate "tectonic" zones where disparate intellectual, judgmental, and decision processes govern. Ignorance of these different mental territories causes all manners of dissonances and category errors in our management of social structures:

> Research hails breakthrough effects; Engineering specifies strength of materials; Manufacturing describe widgets/hour and MTBF[3]; Service calls for FRU's[4]; Finance wants to talk budgets; and the Corporate Office wants to inspire everyone onto a trek into new market opportunity.

The following summary graphic works to situate these disparate resources in a sensorial architecture that we develop more schematically in Appendix A.

---

[3] MTBF: Mean Time Between Failure.
[4] FRU: Field Replaceable Unit.

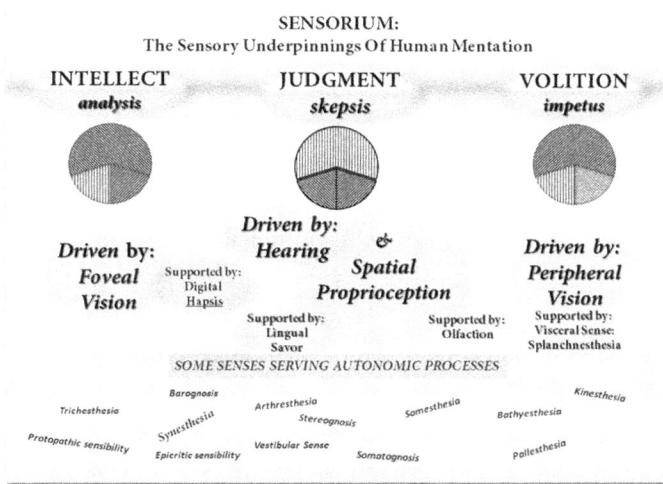

SENSORIUM:
The Sensory Underpinnings Of Human Mentation

INTELLECT
analysis

JUDGMENT
skepsis

VOLITION
impetus

Driven by:
Hearing &
Spatial
Proprioception

Driven by:
Foveal
Vision

Supported by:
Digital
Hapsis

Driven by:
Peripheral
Vision

Supported by:
Lingual
Savor

Supported by:
Olfaction

Supported by:
Visceral Sense:
Splanchnesthesia

SOME SENSES SERVING AUTONOMIC PROCESSES

Barognosis

Trichesthesia

Protopathic sensibility

Synesthesia

Epicritic sensibility

Arthresthesia

Stereognosis

Vestibular Sense

Somesthesia

Somatognosis

Bathyesthesia

Kinesthesia

Pallesthesia

This somewhat granular, *punctuated spectrum* provided to us by our unique sensorium, deeply conditions not only how we perceive the world around us, but also how we project structure into the world we've built up through culture as it emerged from the cellars of instinct.

Because it emanates from the structures of our sensorium, this projected patterning is almost imperceptible to us. We have difficulties seeing ourselves "see"; it is equally troublesome for us to hear ourselves "hear." Our sensorium does not easily support even such elementary self-recursion.

If it is nearly impossible to apprehend them within our own mental operations, they only gradually emerge into view as we move past the encounter with individuals out to the larger groupings of our culture. Once we ascend to the clan and tribe level, these projections begin to etch themselves more clearly into our social reality.

This outbound projection of structural patterns will nonetheless be shown to have fundamental implications for more expansive human exchange environments, and particularly their economic manifestations, our markets.

The Tectonic Boundaries and Zones Within Markets

The major consequence of these patterns is that within the different tectonic zones cleaved out by the projections we are describing, one must find different idioms, divergent vocabularies, disparate analytics, and independent pathways into problems and opportunities unique to each zone.

Moving from one zone to the other requires something of a talent for *protocol conversion* in order for participants in one zone to interact successfully with those in the others. Ignoring this necessary caution will inevitably throw those interactions into category errors and confusion.

We will address these separate institutional domains more at length, but their disparate natures find some resonance in Stephen Jay Gould's philosophical delineation of different "domains of teaching authority," which he dubbed Non-Overlapping "Magisteria" (NOMA).

Gould particularly observed science and religion as separated into such independent spheres.[5] His neologism of *NOMA* is analogous to the separately stacked and layered silo communities and agendas found in every enterprise and institution of any reasonable size and longevity.

The most compelling framing of this projective phenomenon of disparate zones into our exchanges is captured best in this following graphic repeated here from Appendix A:

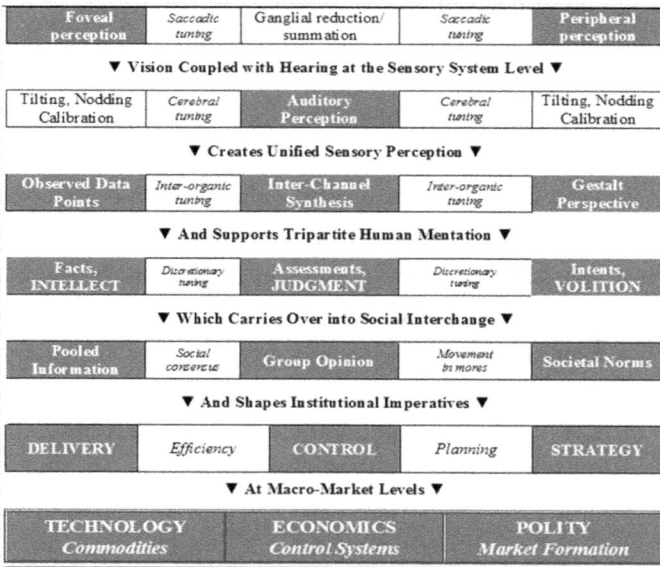

Foveal perception	Saccadic tuning	Ganglial reduction/ summation	Saccadic tuning	Peripheral perception
▼ Vision Coupled with Hearing at the Sensory System Level ▼				
Tilting, Nodding Calibration	Cerebral tuning	Auditory Perception	Cerebral tuning	Tilting, Nodding Calibration
▼ Creates Unified Sensory Perception ▼				
Observed Data Points	Inter-organic tuning	Inter-Channel Synthesis	Inter-organic tuning	Gestalt Perspective
▼ And Supports Tripartite Human Mentation ▼				
Facts, INTELLECT	Discretionary tuning	Assessments, JUDGMENT	Discretionary tuning	Intents, VOLITION
▼ Which Carries Over into Social Interchange ▼				
Pooled Information	Social consensus	Group Opinion	Movement in mores	Societal Norms
▼ And Shapes Institutional Imperatives ▼				
DELIVERY	Efficiency	CONTROL	Planning	STRATEGY
▼ At Macro-Market Levels ▼				
TECHNOLOGY Commodities		ECONOMICS Control Systems		POLITY Market Formation

[5] Gould, SJ. 1999. *Rocks of Ages: Science and Religion in the Fullness of Life.* (New York: Ballantine Pub. Group). Print.

This traces elegantly within human mental processes and their social constructs, the granular, *punctuated spectrum* of mentation[6] that humans range across daily.

It is with this punctuated spectrum of mental operations and their complementary sensory channels noted earlier that we create the exchanges and the world we know. The deep structures of both our mental processes and our sensory channels impose patterns on the outside world in a manner more than a little reminiscent of Plato's effort to describe similar projections in his effort to account for his Universal Forms in the famous *Allegory of the Cave.*[7]

Those structural projections and their pattern languages engrave corresponding fault lines and tectonic zones into our social structures; the most preeminent of which, for our purposes here, are the exchanges in the economic domain we call markets.

These patterns do not betray themselves at the level of primary contact between people. They begin to show up as humans organize into groups that evoke a common quality around which the groups coalesce, as at the clan and tribal level.

Once we reach the level of commercial exchange or economic activity, these patterns begin to dominate and crowd out competing attempts to impose other less deeply based forms: those arising from personal ambition or ideology or antecedent culture.

Taking these primary insights into an inspection of markets, and identifying and describing these fault lines is the primary goal of this book; closely allied to that goal is that of inspecting and mapping the unanticipated tectonic zones, which they delimit.

These goals are important because, if understood and internalized, they can keep other analytical and theoretical work from category errors. These arise from ignorance about the obstacles, these tectonic patterns pose if not accounted for.

---

[6] Throughout this work we use "mentation" because it denotes mental activity in a more generalized sense; this allows us to distinguish within it the more specific, separate powers of **intellect**, **judgment**, and **volition**.

[7] "Selections from Plato's Republic: Book VII, *The Allegory of the Cave.*" www.anselm.edu/homepage/dbanach/repub7.htm (accessed July 23, 2015).

Major Takeaways

Those structural projections and their pattern languages engrave corresponding fault lines and tectonic zones into our social structures; the most preeminent of which for our purposes here are the exchanges in the economic domain we call Markets.

These patterns do not betray themselves at the level of primary contact between people. They begin to show up as humans organize into groups that evoke a common quality around which the groups coalesce, as at the clan and tribal level.

Once we reach the level of commercial exchange or economic activity, they begin to dominate and crowd out competing attempts to impose other less deeply based forms: those arising from personal ambition, or ideology, or antecedent culture.

Taking these primary insights into an inspection of markets, and identifying and describing these fault lines is the primary goal of this book; closely allied to that goal is that of inspecting and mapping the unanticipated tectonic zones, which they delimit.

These goals are important, because, if understood and internalized, they can keep other analytical and theoretical work from category errors arising from the obstacles these patterns pose if not accounted for, thereby greatly accelerating the progress of these other theoretical efforts.

The most persistent effects of these patterns on market operations are those imposed on major decisions and projects undertaken in the enterprises that drive economic activity.

We want now to examine how those projected patterns shape markets, market players, and, more importantly, the rise and demise—the entire natural history—of materiel and service offerings.

To examine these obscure, but overarching patterns, we want to inspect the spectrum that runs from one end to the other of the value offerings they shape. We want to examine a span of Institutional Imperatives we find in any organization enjoying even a short history of operations.

CHAPTER 4

Time-Invariant Market Structure

The Commodities & Breakthroughs Spectrum

To do so, we will want to examine economic-exchange (*market*) offerings familiar to all. And we will want them to help establish *boundary* conditions for the entire set of these market offerings.

These boundary examples will help encompass the wider spectrum of all market offerings, so as to allow for the creation of a taxonomy of such, whether they be service- or materiel-intensive, bleeding-edge technology, or recycled industrial detritus.

The most compelling boundary examples of market offerings are the two domains of *commodities* on one end and *breakthroughs* on the other. Between those two pillars lie every market opportunity humans may encounter.[1]

This polarity has held true from our earliest days. The earliest exchanges of commodity materiel and services would have been the sharing so instinctive among *household* members, as in the classic Greek sense of *economia*,[2] and the extension of that intimate regime out into more

---

[1] It is timely here to note that there is generally a progression in the spectrum that is congruent with the terms *tangible-dominant* at the commodity level to *intangible-dominant* at that of the breakthrough; those specific terms arose from the work of G. Lynn Shostack (1977) quoted in Fisk, R.P., S.J. Grove, and J. John. 2014. "Chapter 2, Frameworks for Managing the Customer's Experience." In *Services Marketing: An Interactive Approach*. (Mason, OH: South-Western).

[2] *Oʼkovoμía*: Attic Greek, household management; also, Singer, K. 1958. Oikonomia: An Inquiry into Beginnings of Economic Thought and Language. S.l.: S.n.

distantly related clans, often using the Gift Economy,[3] taken to such extremities in the Potlatch culture among the Haida and Tlingit tribes of the Pacific Northwest.

Driving contact among more alien groups, early precipitating commodity exchange connections would have involved a grudging awareness of the Golden Goose solution: That co-opting hunters and gatherers for an ongoing portion of their kill or their larder by an appropriate trading exchange, could be a better long-term strategy than murdering them outright only for what they had on hand at that moment. A suspect, alien trading partner is a bit better clan resource than a corpse …

Among the earlier breakthroughs would have been the demonstration that an easily fabricated spear thrower (e.g., *atlatl*) could increase the effective length of a spearman's arm, easily levering the striking power and speed of a thrown spear to velocities close to 100 miles an hour.

It is easy to trace the standard natural history of all breakthroughs in the adoption of such a device:

- Hesitant presentation of a rustic prototype to the leader of the hunt;
- The call for a demo;
- Perhaps even a bake-off against the strongest traditional arm in the clan;
- The trial use of the device in an actual hunt, allowing for rapid dispatching of dangerous prey at a distance, allowing as well for fewer hunting party injuries;
- Discussion of the insertion of this novelty into the received tradition of the hunt;
- Its wary adoption by the younger members of the band;
- Its eventual proliferation and refinement;
- Its later obsolescence against an analogous introduction of the bow and arrow.

Intermediate nodes in the gamut between breakthroughs and commodities could have been catalyzed and even dominated by an

---

[3] Hyde, L. 2007. *The Gift: Creativity and the Artist in the Modern World.* (New York: Vintage). Print.

irruption of value-add **services** rendered by emerging specialists: flint knappers, flensers, tanners, tailors, herbalists, practitioners of basketry and pottery, and later in the onset of agriculture, by owners of threshing floors.

These last become interesting because a threshing floor can easily become a community gathering spot, and can precipitate the formation of informal market spaces and attendant market days. The market days could easily evolve into celebratory events where crop-based cultures versus pastoral or hunting cultures could begin to take shape—all eyed for the main chance by the smarter floor owners.[4]

With just a little muscle,[5] wind, or water power, the floor owner could become as well, the owner and operator of an early mill, where the flavor of the exchange transaction became an overt service—grinding others' grain for a percentage of the yield.

Building out storage bins would make the miller a warehouser and trader. From there to an early bazaar or souq was a short step. Given time, he could enforce his view of future values for the grain he kept on trust, turning him into a maker of value exchanges and markets. At the end of such an evolution, personal wealth and influence could turn the miller into the commercial kingpin of the community.

To explore the modern manifestations of this ancient arena most profitably, it helps to agree on a succinct definition of what a commodity and what a Breakthrough is. Both of them are Exchange Offerings, made of admixtures of value-carrying Materiel and value-producing Service.

Such Exchange Offerings always have an unvarying triplet composition[6] of these three vectors:

---

[4] It is no accident that Egyptian Pharaohs held not only a stylized shepherd's crook, but also a threshing flail as symbols of their power over the two classical cultures of food provisioning: pastoral and cereal husbandry.

[5] The blinded Samson comes to mind: King James Version: Judges 16:21 But the Philistines took him, and put out his eyes, and brought him down to Gaza, and bound him with fetters of brass; and he did grind in the prison house.

[6] For those seeking a salute to more marketing-oriented views of offerings, as in the 4P's of product marketing (*Product/Price/Place/Promotion*) or their extensions in services marketing (*People/Process/Physical Evidence*), I am abstracting here to a higher level, where those attributes are subsumed into one of the three vectors I am using, as they model the tripartite aspects of the Human Sensorium.

- Some value-carrying or value-contributive **substrate**; Materiel, service action, data point, commitment to perform, and so on;
- Some economic dimension of value, cost, or gain; standard **price**, negotiable, promising multiplier on the investment, and so on;
- Some proximity to usability: shelf **availability**, near-line, in Beta, at docking, once tested, and so on.

Using these three parameters, which we call *elemental vectors*, here are the working definitions we will use for our archetypal offerings, Commodities & Breakthroughs:

Commodity

An Exchange Offering of mixed materiel and service components exhibiting an Exchange Offering of mixed materiel and service components exhibiting these elemental *vectors* of *intellect, judgment,* and *volition* within the offering:

- Standard, highly predictable **PRICE** (*driven by vector of judgment*);
- Committed **SHELF AVAILABILITY** (*driven by vector of volition*);
- Standard **QUALITY** (*driven by vector of intellect*).

As of April 24, 2015, the U.S. Commodity Futures Trading Commission was listing 10,350 commodity offerings certified[7] in trade. Each one of them exhibits in unique fashion these three parameters.

---

[7] Stocks of a commodity that have been inspected and found to be of a quality deliverable against futures contracts, stored at the **delivery points** designated as regular or acceptable for delivery by an exchange. In grain, called "stocks in deliverable position." See **Deliverable Stocks**.

Cf. "CFTC Glossary." U.S. Commodities Futures Trading Commission. www.cftc.gov/consumerprotection/educationcenter/cftcglossary/glossary_c (accessed April 24, 2015).

Some Commodity Examples

A gold ingot is a commodity; as is a pork belly; last year's 49 × 68 cm LCD display exhibits aspects of a commodity, because it has stabilized its three aforementioned elemental parameters, as it drifts slowly toward obsolescence. And any medium of exchange, whether coin or currency, is in its lapidary simplicity, a perfect commodity service:

- Value: printed or struck on the surface of the bill or the coin;
- Quality: backed, often by stored gold or silver by the Issuing Government Treasury;
- Availability: In hand, in the safe, in the U.S. Bullion Depository, in the till, or the ATM.

Another compelling example is that of the financial services industry's debt instrument, the **Bond**. Whether we are discussing Muni's, Corporate Junk Bonds, or U.S. Government bonds, these offerings all boil down to an admixture of solely three parameters:

- For **Value**, there is the **Rate** or **Coupon**;
- For **Quality, there is the Rating**, or assessment of the Risk-Worthiness of the bond;
- For **Availability**, there is the **Maturity Date**, establishing the lifespan of the bond.

Sanctions on Commodities

Commodities carry such sharp-edged expectations with them that fudging one of their three parameters can easily throw people into either civil or criminal court:

- Standard Good Delivery gold bars with a 400 troy-ounce weight must exhibit a **quality** of at least 99.5 percent purity. They can be made available only from recognized gold bullion vaults to protect their **availability**. Their **price** is a matter of public record, recorded on futures exchanges worldwide, with variations arising from well-understood arbitrage;

- The **quality** of a carload lot of pork bellies is a matter of inspection by the USDA, with penalties arising from variations that jeopardize public health; contracts for their purchase establish precisely their **availability** to the acquiring food processor, and their **price** again is a matter of public exchange;
- Ciprofloxacin, synthesized for the first time in 1987, is a distinctly effective extension beyond an earlier pharmaceutical. After a series of bruising court cases involving Bayer and others, it is now present in the marketplace as a generic prescription, a pharmaceutical commodity. Its parameters are surveilled in the United States by the Food and Drug Administration. Its **quality** is one that is inspected by visits to the manufacturers; its **availability** is assured by commercial and by governmental stockpiles, especially after the Anthrax alarms of 2001; its **price** varies within a narrow band hedged by market forces well aware of its medicinal value.

Service and Value-Add in the Commodity Context

Commodity items of materiel present themselves to the market with tightly constrained parameters of service enveloping them. If safe **delivery** is assured, and **quality** is well known and certified, and if **price** is within a narrow band of expectations, there is great pressure to avoid blurring things by adding extraneous elements of service onto that basic package.

Bakers of supermarket bread would typically reject wheat with idiosyncratic **qualities**: *fluorescence, hyper*-leavening of loaves to ten sizes larger than normal, wheat that *wanders* afield from the going market **price**, or wheat that is **delivered** *weeks* before it can be warehoused for production.

Buyers may indeed agree to 9- and even 12-grain wheat and grain mixtures, and gluten-free variants. But these must each have won the make or buy contest, and meet market segment expectations; these will enter as foodie niche trends, whose price and availability rapidly settle to commodity bandwidths once their novelty dies away and their market position stabilizes.

This is not to say that relevant service envelopes are not essential and even very costly. The fearsome security surrounding the U.S. Bullion

Depository, and the networked fleets of expensive Brinks and Loomis armored trucks transporting currency, coin, and bullion on our city streets all come as a substantial overhead.

The refrigerated lockers, railcars, and trucking rigs that store and move pork bellies cut down on theft and spoilage loss, but that service envelope is itself both essential and expensive.

The service dimension of a commodity is simply any resource upholding the integrity of one of the three basic commodity attributes: **Quality**, **Price**, **Availability**. This somewhat vestigial presence at the commodity pole undergoes striking growth as we trek up the value-add chain toward breakthroughs and their own triad of attributes as follows.

Breakthrough

An Exchange Offering of mixed materiel and service components exhibiting, again, these elemental vectors of *intellect*, *judgment*, and *volition* within the offering:

- Uncertain but possibly market-making **GAIN** (*driven by vector of judgment*);
- Uncertain but risk-worthy **FEASIBILITY** (*driven by vector of volition*);
- Promising, but barely tested **CRITICAL MASS FUNCTION** (*driven by vector of intellect*) usually delivered as a relatively undifferentiated prototype.

Some Breakthrough Examples

The Cumberland Gap

For a breakthrough to be authentic, it must hold out the promise of a gain not seen before:

- Daniel Boone's obsession with crossing the Cumberland Gap was rooted in the rich **dream** of escaping the overpopulating seaboard colonies, down the five rivers threading the lush Ohio Valley;

- That dream found **feasible** footing in Boone's early forays down the Medicine Trails that crisscrossed that idealized parkland;
- All it needed was men and a mandate to cut even a cursory corduroy road into that wilderness: Boone's **Trace** of 1775 grew to the government Wilderness Road of 1796, and the flow-through of millions of settlers;
- Boone's Breakthrough: imaged; explored; executed; delivered! Priceless!

Others Among Many Breakthroughs

A long-sought 18th century Breakthrough was John "Longitude" Harrison's first, near-perfect Marine *Chronometer*. It solidified seaborne navigation, spawned everbetter versions and brilliant competitors—and entertained brawling lawyers for decades.

The 1903 Wright *Flyer* got us all off the ground, triggered its own better competitors—and launched a Patent War that only the young FDR's tact and swat quashed, in the run-up to U.S. involvement in World War I.

Vanadium,[8] isolated at least twice in the 19th century, was an answer seeking its question until explored, understood, and then legitimized by Henry Ford in its alloy, vanadium steel. Having probed it in his Model N, he went all-in on it in his next, secretive effort. Using it extensively to slash weight and costs, and to boost quality, he made vanadium steel an essential in his grand-slam Breakthrough, the "T." He starred it in promotion, marketing, and merchandising as a Ford value exclusive.

From a dead-stop cold start at the 1908 unveiling of his Model T, the alloy helped fuel the manufacture of 15 million "T's" across 11 countries over 18 years. It helped get us all "out on the road," when there were barely any roads to ride.

The doublet of Dr. Jonas Salk's and Dr. Albert Sabin's polio vaccines were quick-succession Breakthroughs. Facebook's exploding virality is another; NASA's conservatively labeled Evolutionary Xenon Thruster is hoped to be one, bringing closer, human missions to Mars.

---

[8] "History of Vanadium." http://vanitec.org/vanadium/history/ (accessed April 27, 2015).

Successful Breakthroughs may not for quite some time list on any commercial exchange; they arise out of fermenting exploration at many levels: scientific exploration of materiel, services, and systems; social networking; business organization.

Further, Breakthroughs do not find their markets awaiting them—such markets are consequences of the Breakthroughs. The gestation periods can be long—and painful: After a life as a research concept, the awarding of a Nobel, and the usual lawsuits over patents, the laser was first fabricated in 1960; its first real market was the supermarket scanner, introduced in 1974; many felt this an inglorious fate for such a heralded technology; but it opened the flood gates.

Lasers now come in a riot of varieties, and are omnipresent, having made many markets; major sectors of medicine, military, fashion, printing, transportation, and manufacturing have been re-envisioned because of them. Does anyone not know of laser eye surgery?

Among the many splendid venues to view the arrival of technical and scientific Breakthroughs are these two, gauged for the informed lay reader:

- http://phys.org/
- http://www.quantamagazine.org

The most salient characteristic of Breakthroughs is that of their three defining parameters, any can ignite grand obsessions—with no success assured; the Tucker Torpedo, Nicola Tesla's Wardenclyffe Tower, Howard Hughes's Spruce Goose, Fred W. Smith's ZapMail, Google+.

Fever Dreams in the Amazon

An epic example is our ever-intriguing Henry's utopian project of capitalism-cum-welfare, the ill-starred Fordlandia.[9] Here was one Breakthrough dream so intoxicating to the dreamer that other dreams slipped in, creating debilitating cross-talk, and dooming them all to failure.

In that grand scheme, he undertook to monopolize all the rubber production that his worldwide factories might need. Establishing his frontier Fordlandia in the hilly, arid Brazilian outback, he proposed to grow

---

[9] Grandin, G. 2009. *Fordlandia: The Rise and Fall of Henry Ford's Forgotten Jungle City.* (New York: Metropolitan Books).

Southeast Asian rubber trees, tapping their latex for shipment down the Tapajós and the Amazon, out onto the Atlantic, to in-house tire plants closer to market.

He also undertook to mold into striving, upright epitomes of the Calvinist work ethic, indigenous tribes still in bitter rage over the semigenocidal suppression of their Cabanagem Uprising 90 years before by European overlords.

Implacable collisions among locals, imported Barbadians, and American Ford management ended in tragicomic riots, while the increasingly blighted Asian trees withered amid even greater riots of delighted insect hordes and neglect.

His second effort 50 miles closer to the Atlantic at Belterra employed more fertile, level terrain and the use of native Brazilian trees. That struggle would buckle with the onset of synthetic rubber amid the press of World War II.

Fordlandia and Belterra produced great vats of red ink and years of bad press for Ford, but never a commercially significant amount of latex—while 18 weary years dragged on. In 1945, with his father Edsel already two years dead and Henry now senescent, grandson Henry II dropped the axe. The fever broken, Fordlandia lingers now in broken buildings and yellowed archives.

Failures are legion; but attempting Breakthroughs is an essential trigger of societal change: Barry Diller, commenting for the *New York Times* on the failure of the $45 billion struggle in 2015 by Comcast, to acquire Time Warner Cable, said regarding the Comcast owners,

> The differentiator about the Roberts, from almost everyone else they compete with, is that they are always about seizing the next opportunity … You have to be bold enough to reach beyond your current grasp. That sometimes it doesn't work out isn't particularly meaningful.[10]

---

[10] Gelles, D. 2015. "Comcast Withdraws Purchase Bid, but It Isn't Going Anywhere." *The New York Times*, April 24, www.nytimes.com/2015/04/25/business/dealbook/comcast-withdraws-purchase-bid-but-it-isnt-going-anywhere.html?_r=0 (accessed April 27, 2015).

Service and Value-Add in the Breakthrough Context

Breakthrough efforts present themselves to the market with multiple parameters of nonintuitive service enveloping them. Obverses of commodities, Breakthroughs do not promise predictable **delivery**; they imply a substantial component of *invention* (the most rarefied of services). Their successive layers of additive **quality** are very much an implied function of the critical mass success of the invention, and their "**price**" equates to the *value* cocreated with the sponsor of the breakthrough effort. All three of the exchange components are so malleable that the conscious input of the breakthrough team, provider and user, is required to arrive at economic viability and later stability. Thus, service predominates in the provisioning of the breakthrough offering.

Symmetry in Opposition

As we have presented them, the two Exchange Offering sets: Commodities & Breakthroughs, exhibit a fascinating complementarity; they have three congruent parameters, but these three have inverse characteristics; they exhibit *Symmetry in Opposition*:

Symmetry in opposition	
Commodity	Breakthrough
Standard quality ▶	◀ Critical mass function
Price ▶	◀ Gain
Shelf availability ▶	◀ Feasibility

In detail, they parse out in these patterns, evidencing the three critical vectors depicted:

1. The actual Exchange Deliverable:
   - *Commodity*: A passive object, standard, well understood, well niched, surprises not welcome with a service component composed of well-understood responses to known needs;
   - *Breakthrough*: An active initiative, provisionally defined; no existing market; likely with some barely delimited dimensions; potentially a Petri dish of emergent properties; with a poorly defined, but immense space for service and product innovation.

2. Its Value/Financial Dimension:
   - *Commodity*: Hard-edged price; negotiated nose to nose; contracted, whether orally or in writing;
   - *Breakthrough*: Provisionally defined value generally vastly overriding cost estimates, jointly underwritten, and jointly recognized by user and supplier; contracted as a project (perhaps T&M), or partnered as a JV.
3. Its Associated Availability:
   - *Commodity*: Shelf or near-shelf availability; breakage of delivery commitment breaks the deal;
   - *Breakthrough*: "*Give us whatcha got—as you get it! We'll build it out, smooth it in, make it work. If it's piece by piece, we'll still flatten competition!*"

These two archetypal offerings, with their three defining parameters, anchor a span of all offerings in any marketplace; we will develop that span into a taxonomy of offerings. These in sum will reflect a pivotal structure in the architecture of markets in general, rooted back in our discussion of our senses as a tripartite channel for understanding our world and our essential exchanges.

Yang and Yin

Whether the offering in question is a Commodity, or a Breakthrough, or any of myriad modulations in between, the two faces of the offering, Goods (our materiel) and Services are never seen apart from each other; they are a bit analogous to hearing and speech above, "tidally locked" into each other. They constitute a kind of "Tao of the Market," interacting in a complementary fashion as in Daoism's Yang and Yin principles.

Teeter-Totter

Concern for Materiel as a proxy for value predominates over Service at the Commodity end, while Breakthroughs present a powerful mirror image, in that their Service dimensions command the ratio at their end of the spectrum.

	Service			Service		Predominant
Predominant Focus of Commodity Management	Materiel					Focus of Breakthrough Management
▶						◀
				Materiel		

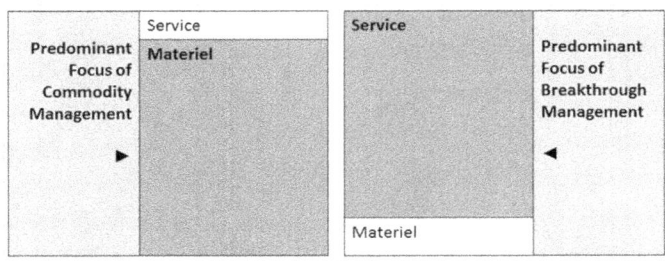

The reasons for this are compelling; commodities are very much known properties; their management is generally efficient, formulaic, reducible to cyclical processes of sourcing, production, storage, movement, payment, and deployment. They pass into vernacular shorthand as "things": Pork bellies, carload lots, puts, calls, ingots, flatbeds, pallets, greenbacks, pig-to-pig pipeline batches, throw-weights, and so on.

Breakthroughs are generally somewhat inchoate, a bit mysterious, and demanding of an outsized amount of novel thinking, analysis, calculation, negotiation—and often the "scheduling" of some ancillary mini-Breakthroughs, driven by great **volition** to get them to work.

This is all **service** territory of the highest order. In vernacular culture they are the prerogative of "Back to the Future" professors with wild hair, of plunging captains of industry (Howard Hughes, Elon Musk?), of semisecret military laboratories (DARPA), of NASA spin-offs, and such.

Another Waypoint in the Commodities & Breakthrough Spectrum

In between the two poles, there is in the manner broached earlier in the section **Markets: Exchanges Unique to *Homo sapiens***, a substantial outbound projection out of our sensory and mental apparatus into large, enduring patterns that help shape the artifacts of our culture.

A major pattern seen repeatedly is that of tripartite division of power in enterprises and institutions. This triplet pattern most clearly endures in the ongoing, static roles surrounding institutional imperatives and business missions. These invariably support the triplet: Service **delivery**, Financial **control**, and Strategic **leadership**.

In business, a somewhat static reading of the institutional hierarchy that is most clear and most germane to our purposes is as follows:

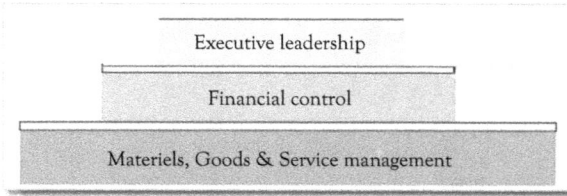

Executive leadership
Financial control
Materiels, Goods & Service management

This classic hierarchy of power actually is challenged daily in the arena of executive ambition and power. Endless struggles are waged, as when underinvestment in product and service lines drives the technology community in a corporation to stage a putsch, to get more focus on pushing the offerings to the forefront of the market.

This may occasion the appointment of a CEO with a heavy engineering background, with him serving until the question before the corporation is no longer in a crisis of technical relevance in the market.

Similarly, if the finance community sees the financial balance of the institution faltering, a finance personality will often ride to the rescue with a refinancing plan, and serve as either de facto or formal CEO until financial rigor is reasserted.

A separate treatment can show that there is a natural history in long-lived institutions[11] of fraught but cyclical handoffs out of one of the three communities over into the next, as the institution confronts the limitations of one or another of the three communities to handle current challenges.

That static view of the hierarchy nonetheless tends to represent a corporation in ideal balance. That tripartite segmentation resonates elegantly with a mapping across our broad categories of materiel, financial control, and organizational intent. And it fits, tongue and groove, with the three major market arenas we have accounted for in the matrix chart cited earlier in Appendix A: The Sensorium Cascades into Markets.

---

[11] Extracts from the Annual Reports spanning the first 80 years of IBM operations vividly shows this to hold imperviously—depression, global war, technology revolutions, notwithstanding. Cf. **Appendix C: Cycles Between Production, Finance, and Market Strategy at IBM**.

	Polity
	Economics
	Technology

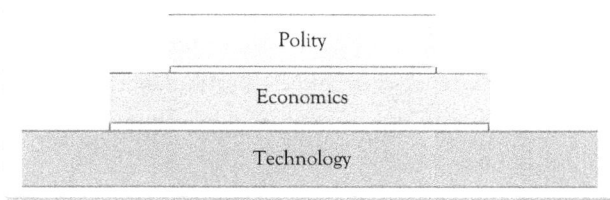

Control Systems: Mediating Commodities and Breakthroughs

If we take the three layers we have established as constituting a generic offering, then each of the three layers can be treated as domains underpinning one of the major institutional imperatives we have discussed: delivery, control, strategy. Our schema can be enriched a bit at this point with CONTROL and its systems artifacts:

	▼INSTITUTIONAL IMPERATIVE▼		
▼OFFERING▼	▼DELIVERY▼	▼CONTROL▼	▼STRATEGY▼
Breakthrough Strategy ►			Critical Mass Function Gain Feasibility
Control Process ►		Integrable Functionality Controllable Outlay Planned Implementation	
Commodity Production ►	Standard Quality Price Shelf Availability		

Control offerings can be parsed out as were those of Breakthroughs and Commodities:

1. The Actual Exchange Deliverable:
   - *Control Offering*: A hybrid; comprising admixed systems, whether manual or automated; procedures for auditing are prerequisites; componentry and logic are often standard, off the shelf, but support emergent service features keeping the acquiring organization in operational and financial balance.

2. Its Value/Financial Dimension:
   - *Control Offering*: Price is usually subordinated into a more comprehensive analysis of price—performance; if the price intrudes on value, vendors will be changed and the acquisition will be rebid.
3. Its Associated Availability:
   - *Control Offering*: The actual control and balance dimensions must come into practical focus for availability to be confirmed. If there are problems with these dimensions, work and acquisition will be extended until the organization's targeted operations can be governed predictably by the acquired system.

While this resultant spectrum does respect its tripartite base, it does not call clearly out two subtle lacunae interspersed among the three main nodes. And business and markets do not operate well with such discontinuities.

As in the instance of human senses, where ancillary senses and cellular summation "fill in the blanks" to tune the gaps among foveal vision, hearing, and peripheral vision, so do there exist interfacial transition zones between product and service management, financial control, and executive leadership.

To help distinguish and define both the three major focal points of institutional activity, and the two intervening transition zones, it becomes important to distinguish between *functions* and *missions*.

Functions Versus Missions—What's Versus How's

For this analysis, we will denote **Delivery** as a stable management *function*; we will so denote **Control** as well, along with **Leadership**. Functions describe institutional constants, standing imperatives, must-do's, "*whats*." All of them imply custody of **authority**.

We will use *missions* on the other hand to denote the two interfacial layers of *efficiency* and *planning*. These we will treat as "*hows*." They are the province of tries-for-fit, feasibility studies, plans and programs, as modulating layers of Ways and Means. These transition zones between the three constants in organizational life again involve *tuning* and adjustment for aptness, feasibility, and effectiveness. Both missions connote constant diplomacy and suasion.

In institutional life, the interfacial zone between Delivery and Control resonates best with **efficiency** and a consultant's entire **word cloud** of its loose synonyms.[12] *Efficiency tunes* how **delivery** and **control** are going to couple. Success in this zone demands **diplomacy**; *authority* is in short supply in the interfacial zones.

The analogous interfacial zone between control and leadership resonates best with *planning* and its own consultant's *word cloud* of loose synonyms.[13] *Planning calibrates* how **control** and strategic **leadership** are themselves going to couple. Success in this zone as well presumes **diplomacy**.

Situating these two interfacial zones as follows allows us now to present a more comprehensive spectrum of Institutional Imperatives:

| DELIVERY | *Efficiency* | CONTROL | *Planning* | STRATEGY |

These five imperatives do not span a featureless expanse. They are **signal flares** flashing which of the imperatives may be in play at different levels of managerial concern. They delimit, as well, the materiel and services in **exchange** that will best support those Imperatives. As such, they are predictors of *exchange* behavior, of inestimable value to seller and buyer, whether of materiel dominant or service dominant.

That fivefold span in sum captures the interim steps in the spectrum we have already sketched out:
Commodities & Breakthroughs©.

We are now at a point in our analysis of the Commodities & Breakthroughs spectrum where we have the endpoints and the medians established. This will later find resonances in Appendix B.

Let us further compare for congruence, the spectra of institutional imperatives versus human mentation we are exploring.

And let us further confirm that correspondence by their novel congruence with yet another deep perspective on human capacities.

---

[12] Adequacy, capability, productivity, competency, cost-effectiveness, suitability, aptness, utility, and so on.

[13] Plan, proposal, motion, organization, schema, proposition, provision, design, suggestion, sketch, project, resolution, system, skeleton, and so on.

INTELLECT	*Interpolation*	JUDGMENT	*Interpolation*	VOLITION

Yields the congruent array:

DELIVERY	*Efficiency*	CONTROL	*Planning*	STRATEGY

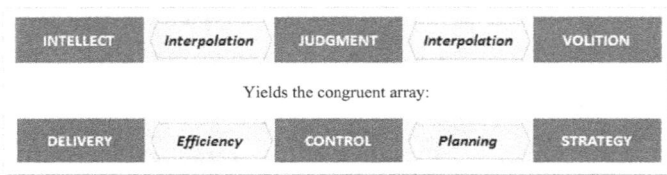

Institutional Analogs to Elements in Maslow's Pyramid

This projection of human capacities up into the social and institutional spaces is most striking in a comparison: the *Human Needs*[14] work of Abraham Maslow compared with the imperatives we find at the institutional level.

Maslow published his *Hierarchy of Human Needs* in 1943, imprinting on most people who read it, his famous hierarchy of five layered sets of subjective imperatives for a meaningful human existence; here is a very schematic extract of its main requirements for successively higher human fulfillment:

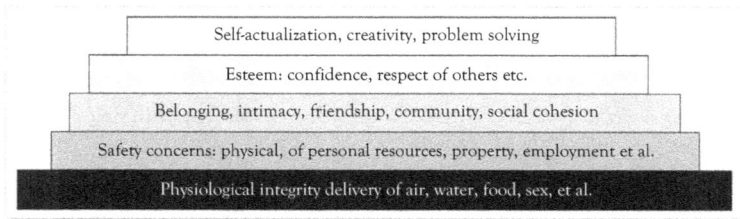

Self-actualization, creativity, problem solving

Esteem: confidence, respect of others etc.

Belonging, intimacy, friendship, community, social cohesion

Safety concerns: physical, of personal resources, property, employment et al.

Physiological integrity delivery of air, water, food, sex, et al.

Maslow himself indicates that the movement up and down these imperatives is fluid, never so clean as it appears in graphics of this sort, however illustrative they may be.

Further, because Maslow was dealing with humans as **subjects**, his indicators are generally indications of **subjective** states: A **sense** of safety liberates a person from **fear**; a **sense** of **belonging** expands a person's **feeling** of healthy **communal context**; an **experience** of applause and acclaim produces an intensely personal **feeling** of being esteemed; and so on.

But examining how these personal imperatives project themselves into the larger institutional spaces requires an abrupt transform in focus,

---

[14] Maslow, A.H. 2013. *Hierarchy of Needs: A Theory of Human Motivation.* (N.p.: Martino Fine Books).

from **subject** to **object**. In this case, the objects are those we call variously, the enterprise, the institution, the venture, or the business.

If organizations may be said to have an interior life, we will understand it as a synthetic derivative only, of the aggregate interplay of human subjectivity in those who are its members. Thus we hear of an army's *esprit de corps*, or a company's morale—both aggregated subjective states of the individual members (there is a world of research rewards awaiting explorers into that domain).[15]

So, when we explore the projection of those personal, **subjective** imperatives Maslow so usefully marked out, up into the institutional world, we leave behind the domain of **subject** and feelings and enter that of **objective imperatives**. And Maslow's various interior, subjective states translate to their analogs in the institution as objective **attributes** of management focus serving the Institutional Imperatives we have discussed.[16]

Musical Chairs and Wheels of Fortune

It becomes important here to address humans moving up and down inside institutional structures from one job to the next. Just as Maslow indicated that humans will migrate, driven along their own unique trajectories among the layers of subjective senses of well-being in his Pyramid, so do humans hesitate, accelerate, and segue in equally opportunistic pathways within the layers of objective institutional imperatives in the tiers depicted here.

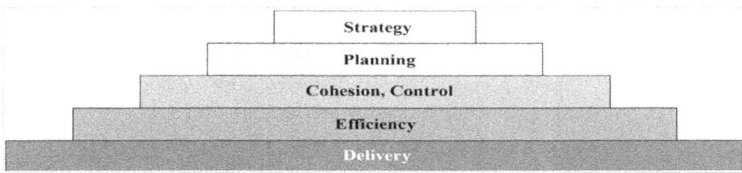

Strategy
Planning
Cohesion, Control
Efficiency
Delivery

---

[15] Here it becomes meet to pay respect to the landmark work of James Grier Miller, who wrote deeply and systematically about the life of entities both of orders far below humans and far overspanning us. His pinnacle work is his splendid volume: Miller, J.G. 1978. *Living Systems*. (New York: McGraw-Hill). Print.
[16] Our ubiquitous DELIVERY, *efficiency*, CONTROL, *planning*, and STRATEGY.

Many technical professionals, carrying along with them an impressive kit of expertise based on the **delivery** of fact-based results, will find it very difficult to "lose my technical competence" by moving into the echelons of management overhead, where an emphasis on *efficiency* rather than **delivery** becomes paramount. Moreover, professionals steeped in financial and operational **control** will sometimes miss the point of leaving details to others, when charged with the broader vistas of strategic market opportunity and revenue **creation**.

More highly volitional natural leaders will find it onerous to "start at the bottom" and work their way up, given their propensity to seize problems as Alexander the Great did, wishing simply to hack apart the various Gordian Knots they find impeding their progress. These personalities will often job-hop, looking for the main chance, to "be in charge." If they stay in one corporation for long, it is largely because it is a culture that allows their players to challenge a number of career ladders during their time with the company. They will nonetheless often blow out at the side, leaving for yet another shortcut to the center of gravity that best suits their own internal imperative: **control, scope of action, or power**.

It can be very entertaining to watch a Type-A volitional leader begrudgingly adopt the protective coloration of a technical or finance type while maneuvering for his chance at the brass ring.

Personalities looking to make their contribution in the areas of quantitative and qualitative assessment will gravitate to the middle tiers and may stay there for long periods while they turn themselves into senior advisors to the office of the CEO, majoring in financial models, reports of financial health, and in guarding the corporation's legal skirts in intense regulatory environments.

The main point to carry away is that the five layers in question are **time-invariant**. They will always be there in any corporation or institution. The professionals in those cockpits, though, rarely fit perfectly, and will tend to mature up from one level to the other, with more than a little drama accompanying that movement. Their later careers may be a downward settling of their earlier progress. It is perhaps reminiscent of the medieval period's favorite career planning graphic, the Wheel of Fortune:[17]

Particularly as it pertains to fitting service profiles to clients in corporations, it becomes of surpassing importance to be alert to what kind of personal imperatives drive the professional who is sitting in which chair, and how those subjective imperatives match to her role amid the objective institutional imperatives, so that the customer's more comprehensive expectations may be met. We will go through a number of filters in the following, to constrain the confusion about what kind of person we're dealing with.

Ya Can't Tell the Players Without a Scorecard ....

In the instance of the institution or the enterprise, the poles of Delivery and Strategy generally fall within the personal experience of even the casual observer. We've all had pizza **delivered**, and we've all seen an NFL

---

[17] Wharton, R. 2012. "Fortune as a Metaphor for the Medieval Church." The Life Death and Afterlife of Geoffrey Chaucer. http://chaucer.lmc.gatech.edu/fortune-as-a-metaphor-for-the-medieval-church/ (accessed August 12, 2015).

coach and his quarterback **strategize** a game through its four quarters, or war movies where the General Staff are all squinting at maps, puzzling out the next phase of the campaign.

When we are talking about Breakthroughs in popular culture, it is generally the colorful genius: Christopher Lloyd, perhaps, in *Back to the Future*. Or Steven Jobs, single-handedly remaking the music business, or Elon Musk, spinning off serial Breakthroughs of market-making dimension.

If we're talking about the Commodity end of the spectrum, it's generally some lone hero or heroine; perhaps the textile worker and unionizer Norma Rae in the movie of that name. Or perhaps the wonderful old Dunkin' Donuts TV ads that showed the donut chef, getting up repeatedly, even in the wee hours, to make the quintessential commodity: donuts.

But when we reach the more interior imperatives of the enterprise, these are not so generally well dramatized. Few blockbuster movies are made about second-line mangers or controllers or functional executives (yawn ...) planning brand extensions.

Generally, malfeasance in implementing environmental, safety, or financial regulations is needed to stoke the drama. When such characters do show up, they're generally vaguely sinister, perhaps tone-deaf "suits," usually helping plot how to further oppress the beleaguered main characters, or how to despoil the ecology.

One memorable instance of this is found in *Avatar*, directed by James Cameron, where two delicious cinematic villains, paid tools of the shadowy Resources Development Administration, work to despoil an Edenic planet of its stores of priceless "unobtanium." The one, Miles Quaritch, the Marine-like security officer, and Parker Selfridge, the venal middle manager, ignore the consequences of killing the ancestral Tree of Souls, grand totem of the indigenous race, the Na'vi.[18] A delicious duo of middle-management malfeasance indeed ...

A marvelous exception relying on the fierce tensions generated by the effort to save lives was that of the depiction of Gene Kranz (played by Ed. Harris) and other NASA staff in the movie, *Apollo 13*. There ordinary techs and a heroic project manager are depicted saving Tom Hanks's James Lovell and the other crew members of that mission, by doing

---

[18] Cameron, J. n.d. "'Avatar' Movie Plot Summary." IMDb. www.imdb.com/title/tt0499549/synopsis?ref_=ttpl_pl_syn (accessed September 28, 2015).

their mundane jobs with a degree of urgent execution bordering on the superhuman.

It becomes important to learn these interior roles rather than to accept their cinematic caricatures. We'll now begin to explore in greater detail each of the generic roles the imperatives call out, and the modes of operation each of the roles elicit, when confronted with quotidian management challenges.

Fleshing Out the Punctuated Spectrum

As a prefatory note, it seems appropriate to use *word clouds* to introduce the projected tectonic spaces dominated by the five Institutional Imperatives we've carved out. Observers of these spaces will come to them from scores of individual professional paths, with differing working vocabularies, and carrying endless nuances at play among their linguistic preferences.

We intend these *word clouds* to rough out the five tectonic zones, rather than to put calipers to delimited plats. In order to avoid too diffuse a badge for each, though, we will, in the interests of concision after this introduction, settle on DELIVERY, *efficiency*, CONTROL, *planning*, and STRATEGY as the shorthand mileposts signifying the five Institutional Imperatives, depicted here as a simple unordered set:

We will now develop the relationships among them all, into an architecture of Institutional Intent, that serves as a systematic *taxonomy* of market structure. We will use this taxonomy to address the larger question of safely, profitably navigating our markets.

A stair-step image of this taxonomy is presented as follows to indicate where we are headed:

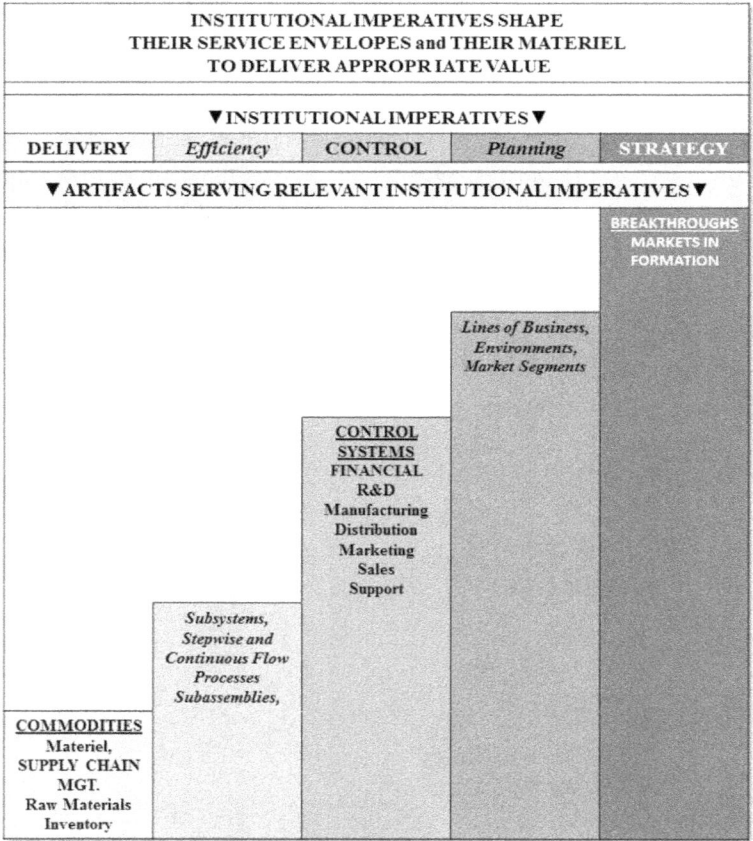

INSTITUTIONAL IMPERATIVES SHAPE THEIR SERVICE ENVELOPES and THEIR MATERIEL TO DELIVER APPROPRIATE VALUE				
▼ INSTITUTIONAL IMPERATIVES ▼				
DELIVERY	*Efficiency*	CONTROL	*Planning*	STRATEGY
▼ ARTIFACTS SERVING RELEVANT INSTITUTIONAL IMPERATIVES ▼				

BREAKTHROUGHS
MARKETS IN
FORMATION

Lines of Business, Environments, Market Segments

CONTROL
SYSTEMS
FINANCIAL
R&D
Manufacturing
Distribution
Marketing
Sales
Support

Subsystems, Stepwise and Continuous Flow Processes Subassemblies,

COMMODITIES
Materiel,
SUPPLY CHAIN
MGT.
Raw Materials
Inventory

The net result of all this structured interaction is a *punctuated spectrum* of value creation, as suggested in the next, more highly developed graphic, which will allow us to expand our taxonomic mapping and further salute Maslow's achievement.

A Taxonomy of the Punctuated Spectrum in Congruence with Maslow's Hierarchy of Human Needs

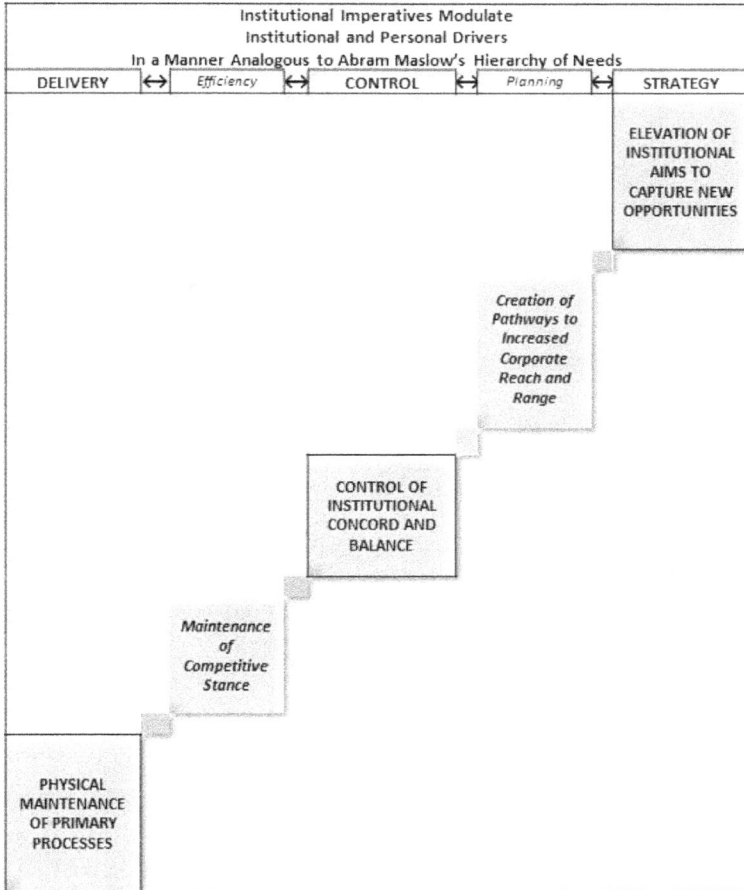

Institutional Imperatives Modulate Institutional and Personal Drivers In a Manner Analogous to Abram Maslow's Hierarchy of Needs				
DELIVERY ↔	*Efficiency* ↔	CONTROL ↔	*Planning* ↔	STRATEGY

ELEVATION OF INSTITUTIONAL AIMS TO CAPTURE NEW OPPORTUNITIES

Creation of Pathways to Increased Corporate Reach and Range

CONTROL OF INSTITUTIONAL CONCORD AND BALANCE

Maintenance of Competitive Stance

PHYSICAL MAINTENANCE OF PRIMARY PROCESSES

The Five Institutional Imperatives: Intent-Driven Cockpits

Each of these five institutional imperatives[19] shows up in the body politic or economic or technical, as specialized subsets of the human sensorium, synthetic *cockpits* with their unique arrays of sensors and levers organized

---

[19] Again: DELIVERY, *efficiency*, CONTROL, *planning*, STRATEGY.

around an overriding **intent**. Such cockpits are broadly speaking, supervisory positions, driven by individuals who are more or less aptly suited to occupy the posts.

Such synthetic cockpits pervade our world far more than we might think; here are just a few random examples from the popular culture, parsed out by salient parameters:

Sensorium	Sensors and inputs	Entities, effects sought	Levers used	Intents served and results desired
USAF F-22 raptor Interceptor Cockpit	Time remaining on station Munitions available Friends or Foes in aerial battlespace Et al.	Foe aircraft Foe SAMS Foe ECM Foe groundresources Friend aircraft Friend ALMS Friend ECM Friend groundresources	Throttle Velocity Direction Aiming Firing HUD nudges Et al.	ID Protection Destruction Collaboration Mission complete
Shakespearean stage space	Eyes Ears Aesthetic sensibilities	Emotional, social insights Humor Pathos Catharsis	Voices Expressions Lighting Music Costuming Color Pacing Dramatic division of action	Sense of closure Elevation to more aspirational level Sense of justice done Comedic relief of anxiety Et al.
Gaming table	Eyes Ears Purported sense of tempo of random Numbers Learned responses to game rules	Player or dealer "tells," Propitious runs of player luck Interim wins to extend playing time	Learned responses to rules of game Available playing money Stamina	Entertainment Sense of mastery over random processes Change of life-changing event
Rodeo bull	Kinesthetic senses Tensed-up back muscles of bull Feedback from bull rope Feedback from rowels on spurs	Elapsed time riding, Safe dismounts Dignified exits	Arm strength Leg strength Muscular reaction time "Seat"	Money rides Championships

Such positions assume a consecrated shape and position in the invariant hierarchy of power and discretion in institutions. To put our five imperatives and their supervisory posts into better focus, we will now delve into each one in succession for a quick snapshot. We will later situate their individual responses to the market in the flow of typical market organization.

The Institutional Imperative of DELIVERY

Delivery is a *primary* Imperative, relying on authority, as opposed to diplomacy. It is the base condition of existence for an exchange, a market,

and for every enterprise that proposes to exist on the value it offers to the wider economic and social spaces it inhabits—that of *demand satisfaction*.

The Delivery cockpit is characterized by its emphasis on *facts*: It drives the professional in charge to concentrate on *certainties*. The broker has either executed the trade at the desired price, or he has not. Manufacturing team members have either produced the night-shift's planned run of deliverable units, widgets, or they have not; quality assurance measurements indicate the refinery has produced the contracted-for 93 Octane gasoline in the latest batch or it has not.

For professionals in the Delivery space, the need to *know* with some certainty what circumstances have been and are present is paramount; accordingly, the space is one wherein *change* is best *suffered* in only a very measured fashion, so as not to upset the need to produce smoothly and consistently those facts on the ground it exists for.

Because delivery in any market comes as an endpoint of some expenditure, *incurring only budgeted costs* is always a key metric in discussions arising in it. The cost can be actual, standard, or variable, but the professional in the Delivery space is wise to know its current value—and to hit it.

There is generally a very low ceiling for initiative in the Delivery space; initiative implies *change*, which always carries with it some dimension of upset and surprise.

Because there is so much emphasis on already-structured delivery systems at this level, the artifacts the Delivery professional manages are overwhelmingly **commodities**, whether as structured service offerings or as batches or runs of materiel.

The Institutional Imperative of EFFICIENCY

Efficiency is a *subordinate* Imperative, relying on diplomacy and suasion, as opposed to authority. It is the recurrent exploration of modest change for modest gains in quality or cost avoidance. It is the means for an exchange, a market, and for market players, to improve marginally, the quality of the process of cocreating value within established processes.

The *Efficiency* cockpit is characterized by its exploration of *increments of change*: The broker has executed the trade at the desired price, but could he be doing so at less cost, or with increased client satisfaction? Manufacturing team members may have produced the night-shift's planned run of deliverable units, widgets, but could quality assurance step in and measurably point out how to improve the yield out of each process run?

For professionals in the *Efficiency* space, the need to *project* with some assurance what incremental changes can be made safely is paramount; accordingly, the space is one wherein *change* is best metered into the flux of process and materiel flow in a very measured fashion, so as to minimize risk and allow for early capture of benefits: costs avoided, quality incrementally improved, and so on.

Because *Efficiency* in any exchange process comes by the investment of some resource, *a simple ROI* is generally an imperative in proposing and tracking investment at this level.

There is generally a tightly circumscribed call for initiative in the *Efficiency* space; established processes must be kept intact, and flows of materiel must be undisturbed, with mainly incremental improvements the hallmark of success in this area.

Because there is the injection of incremental change in the processes found at the *Efficiency* level, the offerings will generally have a novel component (e.g., better service response and improved subassembly) catalyzing that *efficiency* boost. These can be an optimization of delivering a service offering, or of delivering a marginally improved quality of materiel, or some other parameter lifting the offering a bit out of the raw **commodity** level.

The Institutional Imperative of CONTROL

equate offset
compensate level
square weigh counteract
match counterbalance harmonize

CONTROL

set
steady **BALANCE**
poise parallel adjust equalize
neutralize even redeem
accord stabilize attune
readjust correspond

CONTROL is a *primary* Imperative, relying on authority, as opposed to diplomacy. It is the base condition of *equilibrium* for an exchange, a market, and for every enterprise that proposes to exist on the value it offers to the wider economic and social spaces it inhabits.

The Control cockpit is characterized by its emphasis on *quantitative and qualitative rigor*: sales, engineering, production, or other functions have either met their key performance indicators (KPI's), or they have not. The budget targets published to each function have been met, overrun, or undershot. It is up to the Control layer of management to arbitrage among the variances those functional units report, to maintain corporate or divisional equilibrium. If there is a substantial problem, the Control management must inform higher levels of management of the problem, and participate in the remedies available to those offices.

For professionals in the Control space, the need for clarity to support financial *load balancing* among performance trends that are underway is paramount; the space is also one wherein incessant *change* is best anticipated and managed within the parameters available from internal enterprise resources first.

There is generally wide latitude for initiative in the Control space; established processes and subsystems can be examined for replacement, so long as the ROI carries the case for reduced or avoided **costs**; vendors of materiel can be challenged and replaced, and operational partners can be added or dropped in the interest of a better balance of **costs** against tracked revenues. Generally though, professionals at the Control level do not have wide scope for expanding revenue.

Offerings at the Control level are generally at the operational system level, with subsystems, manpower, materiel, and operational doctrine all targets for the balancing of costs against likely revenues.

The Institutional Imperative of PLANNING

Planning is a *subordinate* Imperative, relying on suasion and diplomacy, as opposed to authority. It is the base condition of injecting major change for an exchange, a market, and for every enterprise that proposes to exist on the value it offers to the wider economic and social spaces it inhabits.

The *Planning* cockpit is characterized by its preparation and presentation of *quantitative and qualitative projections,* best depicted as *alternative scenarios*: sales, engineering, production, or other functions with their various KPI's, are all grist for the mill of *planning* the enterprise into the next phase of market penetration, or of market formation.

The financial perspective at the *Planning* level shifts to the preparation of After Tax Discounted Cash Flows predicated on the institution's Internal Rate of Return. Earnings Before Interest, Tax, Depreciation and Amortization (EBITDA), actual and pro forma, becomes of surpassing importance, as do Asset-based and Comparable Market Analyses; income and cash flow analysis is always a part of such *planning*.

For professionals in the *Planning* space, the need for an understanding of market trends that underpin the scenario work is paramount; the space is also one wherein substantial *change* within existing markets is called for, and where external resources arising from mergers, joint ventures (JVs), and new financing is well within the scope of work.

There is generally wide latitude for initiative in the *Planning* space; entire functional systems and operating environments can be examined for replacement, so long as the ROI carries the case for the **expansion of revenue** from *existing markets*; vendors of materiel can be challenged and replaced, and operational partners can be added or dropped in the interest of a better balance of **revenue growth** versus planned cost structures.

Offerings at the *Planning* level are generally at the functional system level, with all subsidiary resources: manpower, materiel, and operational doctrine legitimate targets for the expansion of existing **revenue streams** against likely expenditures and investments.

The Institutional Imperative of STRATEGY

STRATEGY is a *primary* Imperative, relying on authority, as opposed to diplomacy. It is the base condition for the forceful expansion of an existing exchange, a market, and for the reach and range of every enterprise that proposes to exist on the value it offers to the wider economic and social spaces it inhabits. It stands or falls on its ability to create demand.

The Strategy cockpit is characterized by its emphasis on *vision*: Successful CEOs generally leave *problem* solving to the COO personalities, and concentrate on *opportunities*. One does not create entirely new revenue streams, and bring online, entire new markets by solving problems with existing environments.

To accomplish this direction setting, the corporate Strategist learns quickly how to canvass all the major KPIs that could dislodge him or her, and how to keep everyone responsible for them on a relatively short leash. Once that is learned, the Strategist delegates that mule-skinner role to the COO personalities, and begins to work with the more visionary staff to crack open new opportunities. These can be financial, technological, geographical, or socioeconomic.

Where the less-encompassing levels of management attention have had a fraught relationship with change, the Strategy executive must make change his best friend. No one keeps a CEO position by promising stasis.

Initiative in this arena is described in JVs, in Breakthrough initiatives intended to break existing market paradigms, and in takeover ploys aimed at denying arenas of opportunity to potential competitors. Stock prices, cost of capital, financial break-evens are all gauges on the CEO's dashboard indicating just how far the corporate tachometer may be pressed past the red line in the pursuit of a new level of corporate performance.

Some Parameters Through Which Institutional Imperatives Cycle

We will now populate a number of organizational and professional parameters through our market spectrum, with an eye to laying more and more detail into the special niches occupied by each of the five institutional imperatives. Each of these niches call out different business resources, and their imperatives demand that the professionals serving within their boundaries "play by the rules" pertaining to the niche in question.

These all become evidence for how to perform, and to succeed, whether it is working, making, buying, selling, servicing, *planning*, managing, or leading.

To forecast where we are going, these are a few of the parameters we could probe on how our market players differentiate themselves when in the confines of one of the five institutional imperatives:

Financial Effect Tuned to Each of the Five Imperatives
Attitude Toward Change Tuned as Above
General Stance on Work as Above
Language Orientation as Above
Quantitative Vocabularies as Above
Contract Paper as Above
Aggregating Tools as Above
Response to Heavy vs. Light Industry Regulation as Above
Examples: Telecommunications Industry
Examples: Casino Table Games Industry
Example: Some Regulatory Agencies
Example: etc.
Example: etc.

This list of attributes is only suggestive; once one becomes accustomed to the five institutional imperatives, they become discrete sets of lenses through which offerings, whether service-dominant or materiel-dominant, may be examined and understood; further alternative examples are legion.

Ad hoc taxonomies can be undertaken, adding on further parameters that display the operational, buying, and selling behaviors of players in the institution or the enterprise in question. This analysis becomes a sieve, sifting out what a service/materiel combination must contain to meet the objectives of the client once her objectives have been properly parsed out.

Financial Effect

The premier touchstone of this multiple analysis will be Financial Effect, modulated across each of the five Institutional Imperatives:

- Delivery-oriented first-line management punches out the offering: loans booked, widgets crated and palleted to the loading dock, hash slung, properties sold, apps downloaded, and so on. The proper financial focus of first-line

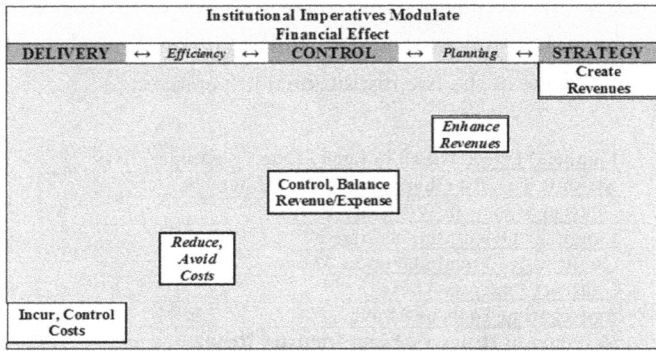

management is to get the offering[20] **delivered**, incurring only the costs allocated in the budget, and have an excellent story when costs rise beyond budget allocations.

Visibly focusing on reducing or avoiding costs will often earn the manager a nudge to get back to "cooking the donuts." Ambitious newbies will have to work hard first to get those donuts out of the door, and then ask for a hearing on ideas about improving the bottom line.

- Intermediate managers focus on incremental "better ways," getting more for less, with a bit more *efficiency*. If they can hone a process to drop utility costs; if they can replace a supplier with a less costly source—control. They want intense—that's a win for them. Intermediate management, less concerned with last week's run, can look out a bit and try to anticipate shifts in supply, to better position the company by **avoid**ing costs.
- Executives charged with maintaining financial clarity and control for an institution are looking always to **control** trade-offs inside a company, to keep the overall budgetary plans in play and reflective of the company's strategic intent. They will move resources in and out of budgetary accounts, as the business cycle shifts their booked plan. Their KPI[21]

---

[20] As always, the offering can be "service dominant" or "materiel dominant."
[21] KPI: Key Performance Indicator.

is always to maintain the committed plan so as to deliver predicted or better results for the institution.

- *Planning* professionals engage in taking the concerns of executive and control-level management about the yields out of **existing** product and service lines and whole lines of business, to study how more revenue can be extracted by materiel and service line extensions, by penetration of those lines into new geographies, and by blending in complementary lines from partnering corporations. All of this requires study, consultation, and ***planning***. Often times, these efforts are led by functional executives tasked to see them to completion by the corporate office.

In a grand example a few years ago that played right into its strategy of keeping its equipment and provisioning strategy focused against its markets, Southwest Airlines planned for and bought fuel futures[22] when few others thought that was judicious; it paid off handsomely when the cost of jet fuel later spiked, and Southwest's fuel cost per passenger gave them great pricing power over their competitors who were not *planning* for such market shifts. Revenues jumped, even though the focus was on maximizing their position in **existing** markets.

- Executive management is properly concerned with the next play; the next marketplace, the next revenue creation project. Today's algorithm of success has in it tomorrow's obsolescence and decline. No CEO keeps his job by saying "I'll keep things just the way they are during my tenure." If there is no new source of revenue in sight, it's time to replace the CEO with a leader with a still-burning appetite for change ...

---

[22] "The Secrets of Southwest's Continued Success." 2012. *The Economist*, June 18, www.economist.com/blogs/gulliver/2012/06/southwest-airlines (accessed May 06, 2015).

The matrix and subsequent previous discussion constitute a format we'll use to explore other aspects of marketplace segmentation, so as to flesh out the **five distinct business imperatives** against which services and materiel can be compared for most appropriate purchase, use, sale, and support.

It becomes important to emphasize yet again that management operating in one or another of these Imperatives will generally encounter translation difficulties in sending messages most bound up with his or her own focus. No one speaks across all five Imperatives equally fluently.

This difficulty in moving messages across boundaries creates endless impasses in institutional life where category errors crop up in the face of mutual incomprehension arising from imperfectly understood shop talk, professional terms, and imperatives not well understood across layered boundaries.

Return to List: Some Parameters Through Which Institutional Imperatives Cycle.

Attitude Toward Change

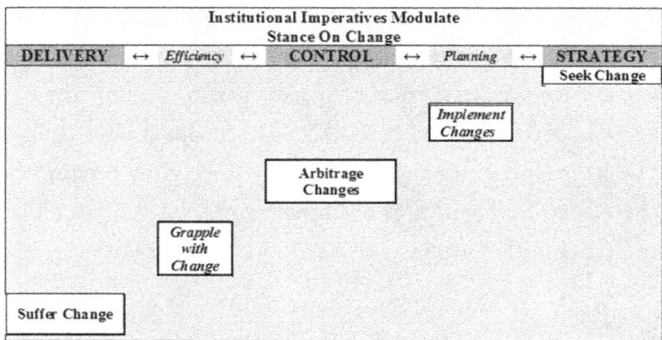

- In their role of administering the DELIVERY of the basic product and service line items, first-line managers **do not easily absorb** new directions or change items coming from superiors, customers, or regulatory bodies. Because they acclimate themselves to optimizing a known delivery process, anything that jeopardizes that internalized process may be seen as a compromise of **delivery**;

- Managers at the intermediate *Efficiency* levels have a love–hate affair with change; their path to recognition and advancement is that of introducing **incremental** improvements to the processes and subsystems they administer. But **strategic** change can wipe out levels of intermediate management[23] far more often than that of first-line management or the levels above;

- Executives at the CONTROL level have an ongoing task of keeping the institution literally, **in balance**. Accordingly, they maintain surveillance on the budgetary process to maintain the overall commitment to the plan booked for the financial period ahead. When the inevitable alterations to the plan crop up, they work to redistribute assets and commitments enough to keep the plan intact. If the plan shows signs of serious compromise, they participate in the executive discussions undertaken to decide on a new strategy;

- Functional executives and *planning* staffs are at the disposal of the CEO and her office to turn their strategic direction into executable plans. Accordingly, **accepting and implementing change** is very much in their wheelhouse; it is where they can make the greatest impact, and distinguish themselves for further opportunities;

- Chief Executive Officers must be **impatient for change**; as stated earlier, a CEO is in that role because the institution must be actively open to changes in STRATEGY or find itself receding into backwater markets with no prospect for the future.

Return to List: Some Parameters Through Which Institutional Imperatives Cycle.

---

[23] Lam, B. August 27, 2015. "The Secret Suffering of the Middle Manager." *The Atlantic*. Atlantic Media Company, Web. August 31, 2015.

General Stance on Work

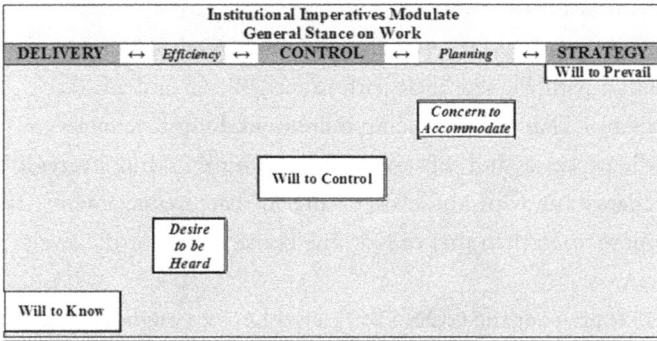

Institutional Imperatives Modulate General Stance on Work								
DELIVERY	↔	*Efficiency*	↔	**CONTROL**	↔	*Planning*	↔	**STRATEGY**

(diagram)

Will to Prevail

Concern to Accommodate

Will to Control

Desire to be Heard

Will to Know

- First-line, DELIVERY-oriented managers want most of all, to **know** with as much **certainty** as possible, the parameters defining their work; confusion and uncertainty imply the possibility of unanticipated change, and that surprise opens the door to some risk and failure in getting the deliverable out, whether it be materiel-dominant or service-dominant.

  This is most critical when lives are at stake; police and fire departments generally post quite rigid Plans of the Day to ensure that there is clarity about who is scheduled in, what equipment is off-line, and what the conditions of unrest or potential fire are out in the community.

- Intermediate management has a different concern; they want a forum for what they see as areas for the kind of **incremental improvements** in *Efficiency* they are authorized to undertake. They have the experience from watching first-line supervisors work to get the deliverables out, and see ways to get more efficiencies. These may be through upgrades of equipment, through improved workflows, or through reworking one or more elements of the product or service lines. Whatever it is, they almost always have to marshal a constituency to get their propositions executed.

- CONTROL level executives—control. They want intense quantitative and qualitative feedback from all compass points, so that they may keep the ship on course and steady, as per the demands of the CEO. It is more important to them to keep all elements of a plan in **cohesion** than it is to attack particular elements of booked plans for marginal improvement.
- Functional executives and senior planners are generally more interested in examining and *planning* how best to bring in **more revenue** out of the current mixes of market to offering.
- STRATEGY-level executives, CEOs and members of a corporate office all want to know what markets can be opened next, and what governmental and financial constraints need to be understood and negotiated in order to open those up. They are fixated on **strategies** for the ***creation* of revenues** rather than the laudable, but still less ambitious goals of maximizing *existing* streams.

Return to List: Some Parameters Through Which Institutional Imperatives Cycle.

Language Orientation

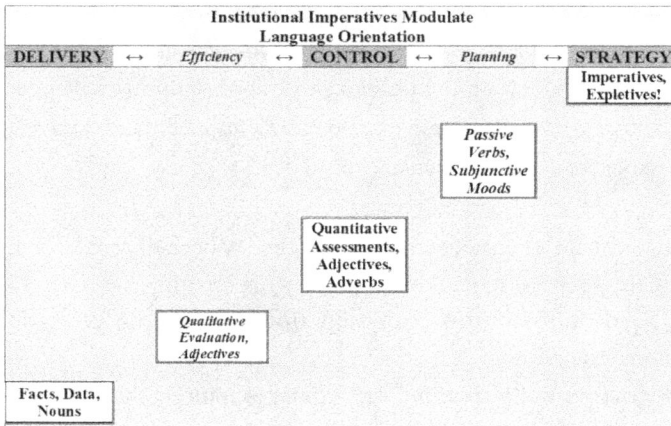

It is striking how individual institutional imperatives find resonances within the syntax of the language used to manage them.

- Professionals operating in the DELIVERY layer will invariably focus their vocabulary on discrete items, as opposed to attributes. Nouns will pepper their speech, as well as measurements and constants.
- Those operating in the *Efficiency* layer will focus more on modifiers that identify either an eroding or an improving condition associated with the items found at the Delivery level; accordingly, adjectival modifiers will occupy much of their running commentary. When analysis is called for, straightforward quantitative and qualitative analysis of existing conditions is the norm.
- At the CONTROL level, most executives will be adopting an even more complex syntax, depending on a full range of modifiers: adjectives, adverbs, with comparative analyses and alternative scenarios beginning to emerge.
- At the *Planning* level, professionals deal almost constantly in the currency of scenario *planning*, alternative financial modeling, and min, med, and max *planning*; because of their proximity to the Corporate office, their language tends more toward the passive voice.
- At the STRATEGY level, there is a great premium on the active and the emphatic, even the *imperative* mood. When not confronted with microphones and "tape at 10pm" challenges, strategy-level professionals often relish an incendiary and expletive-laden vernacular.

This athletic orientation does not take away their need for deeply researched policy alternatives, especially in mature industry settings where regulation has grown into and around preceding generations of entrepreneurial effort.

The telecommunication industry comes to mind in this context; laden with lobbying and regulatory compliance concerns arising from over a century of operation, C-level execs in this industry demand deep staff work before they venture into whatever uncharted waters appear next. (Nonetheless, the bias toward fearsome atmospherics in those suites is legendary.)[24]

Return to List: Some Parameters through Which Institutional Imperatives Cycle.

Quantitative Vocabulary

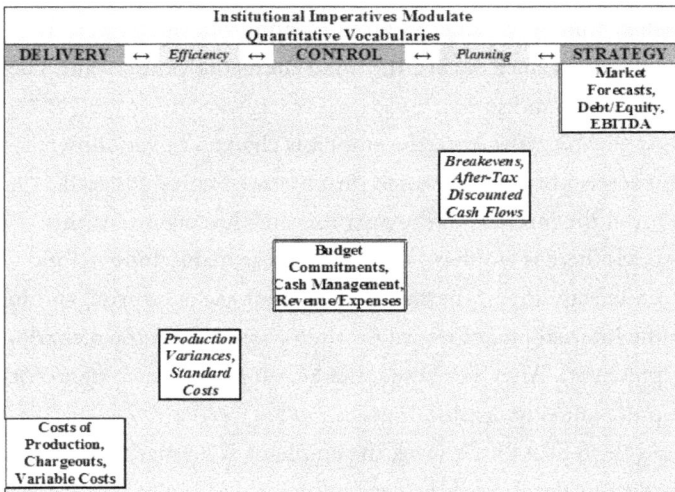

Institutional Imperatives Modulate Quantitative Vocabularies				
DELIVERY ↔	Efficiency ↔	CONTROL ↔	Planning ↔	STRATEGY

At each distinctive level, the language of analytics changes. It becomes of great importance in designing control and management systems for these, to acknowledge the disjunctures that exist when jumping from one level to the next.

- At the DELIVERY level, analytics exist to capture definitively, whether production of service events, or of manufactured widgets occurred on plan. This is always a retrospective exercise, capturing recent history. The metrics are generally those of quantities produced, and dollars expended versus standard or actual allocated cash.

---

[24] "Suit Against Southwestern Bell in 4th Week of Trial." n.d. *The Times-News—Google News Archive Search. The Times News*, Hendersonville, NC. Web. September 07, 2015.

- At the *Efficiency* level, the analysis becomes more one of comparing between current performance and the improvements to existing delivery systems that may be made to decrease costs. These tend to be straightforward spreadsheet exercises extending trends out for periods matching the useful life of the proposed cost improvements.
- At the CONTROL level, the vocabulary changes again to that of depicting stability and the balance required for reporting to stakeholders, whether in profit or nonprofit operations. These include Balance Sheets, Income Statements, Sources and Uses of Funds, and so on.
- At the *Planning* level, the emphasis changes to various what-if's, scenarios, down which the enterprise could proceed, given the interests of the organization's leadership. At this level, there is emphasis on such tools as maintaining a solid understanding of the cost of capital for the enterprise, and for the internal rate of return for the various legs of the scenarios presented. After Tax Discounted Cash Flows are *de rigeur* for profit-making organizations.
- At the STRATEGY level, the emphasis is on market forecasts, cost of capital, stock prices, and the whole panoply of external financial analysis. By and large, it has become a rule that, in addition to the price of common stock associated with the institution in question, the C-level suite of management will have ready to hand the EBITDA of the for-profit institution.

  Executives managing not-for-profit institutions will have ready to hand the results of asset-based analyses, comparable market analyses, and income or cash flow analyses.

Return to List: Some Parameters through Which Institutional Imperatives Cycle.

Contract Paper

- Generally, at the DELIVERY level, exchanges are effected through fixed prices; there may be some negotiation

Institutional Imperatives Modulate Forms of Contract Paper								
DELIVERY	↔	*Efficiency*	↔	**CONTROL**	↔	*Planning*	↔	**STRATEGY**
								Partnering JV's Retainers
						Project Proposals, Turn-Keys		
				Standard Contracts, RPQ Inclusions				
		Purchase Orders, Position Letters						
Sealed Bids, Spot Trades								

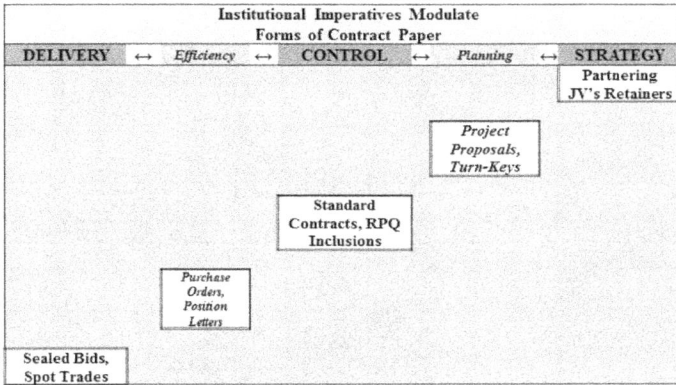

beforehand, but there is a certainty about the price associated with commodities, whether in the mode of materiel provisioning or in the delivery of services.

This is effected through price tags, or through sealed bids or spot trades, but there is a hard-edged aspect to the assertion of value by the provider. The consumer generally has a yes or no response to this form of value presentation.

- At the *efficiency* level, things become more fluid; there are generally negotiations based on the quantity of subassemblies or in the number of loaded man-hours of service to be included in the billing from the provider. If there are delivery constraints, there may be position letters to be executed, and purchase orders to be completed for tracking by both the buyer and the seller.
- At the CONTROL level, there may be special engineering and development tasks aimed at integrating ancillary function into various control systems, with these services requiring add-on contractual agreements.
- At the *Planning* level, there will be project proposals based on plans that could have been jointly developed by buyer and seller, with unique services and materiel codeveloped, to be produced under a performance contract that may be a turn-key.
- The STRATEGY level calls routinely for contract paper that defines market-level partnering, even to the depth of outright JVs, with capital infusions from one or the other side.

Return to List: Some Parameters through Which Institutional Imperatives Cycle.

Aggregating Tools

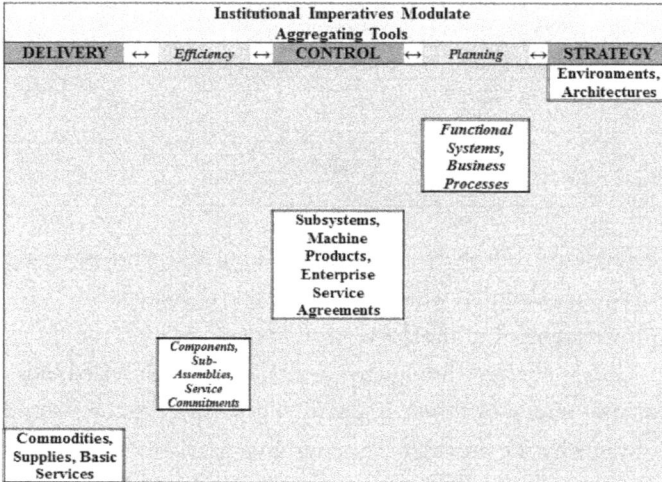

It becomes of surpassing importance here to understand that all the artifacts populating this *punctuated spectrum* are tools; tools, literally, serve to engender value, cocreated and validated between the maker and the user of the proffered tool, whether that be a service action, a materiel object, or an intellectual object.

These tools follow an evident path of the buildup of increasing complexity as they are aggregated to serve the creation of ever-more complex offerings of value to provider and user. At the bottom, in the realm of Commodities, they are simple examples of known makeup, offered at a known price, possessed of a known quality.

At the upper reaches of Breakthroughs, they can be entire environments, often spanning continents and countries, and offering entire architectures and cultures of service provision. At one end can be a small box of McDonald's fries; at the other end are the international social networks of providers like Facebook and LinkedIn, or the telecommunications network environments provided by cooperating companies like AT&T, British Telecom, and France's Orange S.A. These last cooperate through the aegis of the International Telecommunications Union. We will explore such regulators next.

Return to List: Some Parameters through Which Institutional Imperatives Cycle.

Response to Heavy Versus Light Regulation

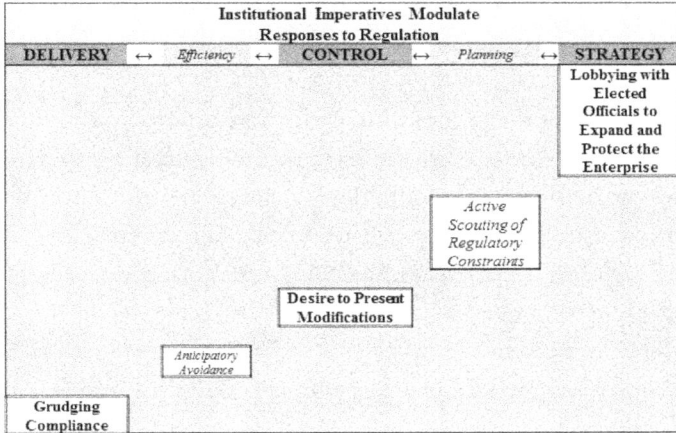

Institutional Imperatives Modulate Responses to Regulation				
DELIVERY ↔	*Efficiency* ↔	**CONTROL** ↔	*Planning* ↔	**STRATEGY**
				Lobbying with Elected Officials to Expand and Protect the Enterprise
			Active Scouting of Regulatory Constraints	
		Desire to Present Modifications		
	Anticipatory Avoidance			
Grudging Compliance				

Because regulators have the power to demand change, the relationship between the occupant of the cockpit in question is congruent with that of general Attitude toward Change.

Please Return to List: Some Parameters through Which Institutional Imperatives Cycle.

Examples: Telecommunications Industry

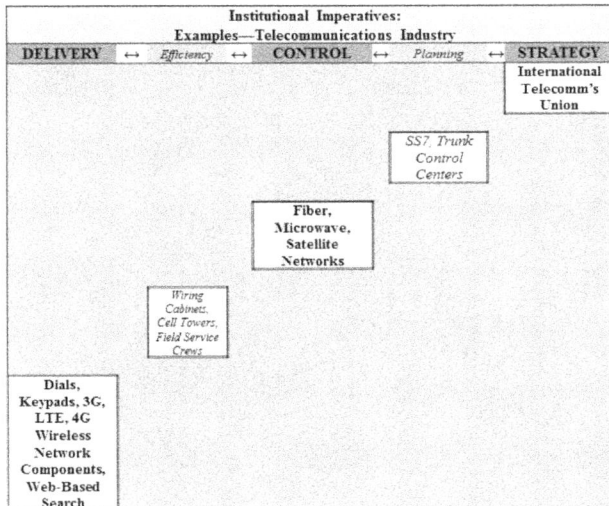

Institutional Imperatives: Examples—Telecommunications Industry				
DELIVERY ↔	*Efficiency* ↔	**CONTROL** ↔	*Planning* ↔	**STRATEGY**
				International Telecomm's Union
			SS7, Trunk Control Centers	
		Fiber, Microwave, Satellite Networks		
	Wiring Cabinets, Cell Towers, Field Service Crews			
Dials, Keypads, 3G, LTE, 4G Wireless Network Components, Web-Based Search				

The telecom industry, long matured around the base technologies of switched networks and endless miles of copper wire, has undergone radical change in the years since acoustic couplers and later microwave began to challenge traditional copper; Carterphone in 1959 and MCI in 1968 began to breach Theodore Vail's 1907 "One System; Universal Service" rationale for monopoly; and the digitizing and packetizing of data began its relentless march forward.

While each of the previous five nodes have seen successive invasions of superseding technologies, the hierarchy of aggregating service tools around progressively more ambitious architectures and environments remains robust. The preceding stairstep has radically different incumbents in every cell, but the overall architecture of tools in service to a population that uses communication to produce social, economic, political, and value remains the same.

Return to List: Some Parameters through Which Institutional Imperatives Cycle.

Examples: Casino Table Games Industry

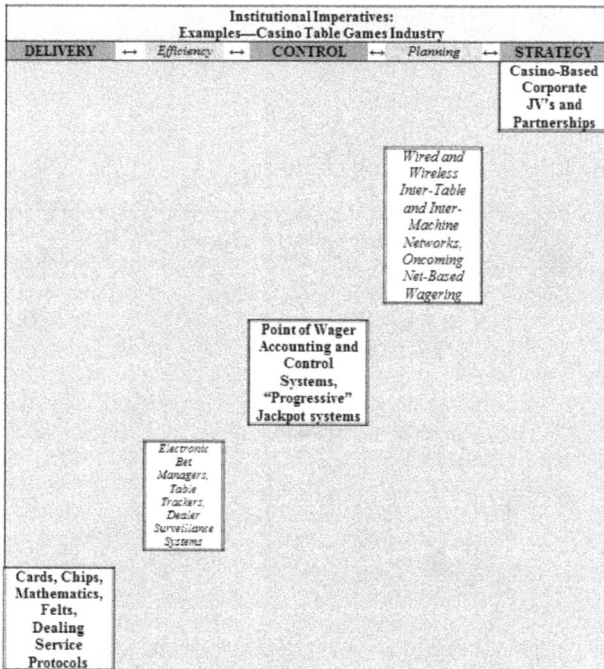

There are only three basic services that the gambling (euphemistically relabeled "gaming") industry provides in return for relieving the gambler of discretionary income:

- Entertainment: Architectural glitz, pinball wizard lights and sounds, drink attendants in becoming attire, and so on;
- "Skill": The specious chance to assert the superiority of "table smarts" or "reading the slots" over random number generators feeding fixed algorithms favoring the house over the longer run;
- The generally remote possibility of securing a "life changing event," a jackpot of epic size.

The one constant in the casino environment underpinning this environment is that of service: Keeping the player at the table or the machine, playing through proffered drinks, snacks, and allowing for bathroom breaks with TITO (Ticket/In—Ticket/Out) chit systems accounting for positions before and after those breaks.

If a machine or a table breaks down, there are usually FRUs (Field Replaceable Units) in the Pit Boss's area, where online diagnostics will tell the attendants what part to replace, to get the POW (Point of Wager) back up and running so as to relieve more gamblers of their weightier wallet contents.

If the FRU strategy fails, a quick telephone or text to the supplier of the machine or table will either retrieve service techs out of their onsite cubby holes in the casino for a quick repair and restart, or, in the worst case, an entire table assembly and a tech may be overnighted from the nearest inventory depot.

It is this commitment to relentless 24/7 availability of their entertainment producing product that allows even a mediocre gaming station (machine or table) to keep its place in the casino real estate, grinding out the casino's revenue, its "hold," or conversely, the player's "drop."

If this full-tilt vendor support of the online, available POWs is in good health, all the other amenities offered by the casino can add in their value offerings to the player: food, entertainment, comfort, excitement, release, dream-chasing, afterglow, memories. Without it, there is no casino; there is only perhaps a very expensive hotel, variety show, restaurant, or night club. In that deathless phrase from American advertising; in that instance the cry could be raised, "Where's the beef?"[25]

Return to List: Some Parameters through Which Institutional Imperatives Cycle.

Example: Some Regulatory Agencies

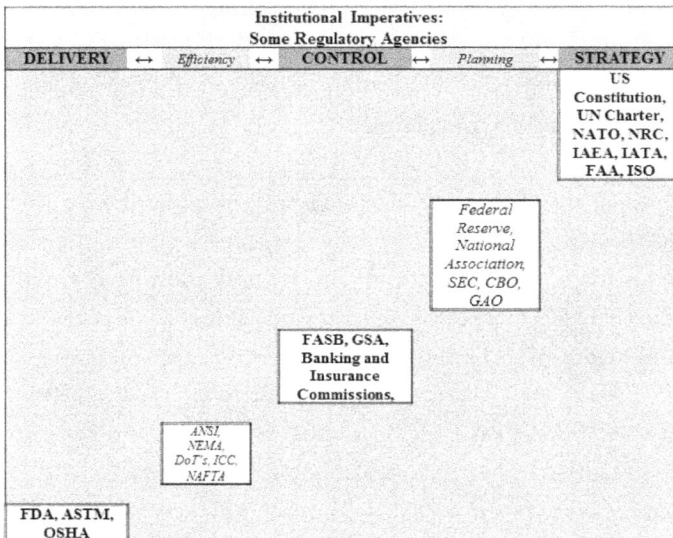

		Institutional Imperatives: Some Regulatory Agencies						
DELIVERY	↔	*Efficiency*	↔	**CONTROL**	↔	*Planning*	↔	**STRATEGY**

US Constitution, UN Charter, NATO, NRC, IAEA, IATA, FAA, ISO

Federal Reserve, National Association, SEC, CBO, GAO

FASB, GSA, Banking and Insurance Commissions,

ANSI, NEMA, DoT's, ICC, NAFTA

FDA, ASTM, OSHA

It becomes important to parse out regulatory bodies based on their interest in one or more of the Institutional Imperatives. For example, the United States Food and Drug Administration has as its mission statement the DELIVERY of the following:

FDA is responsible for protecting the public health by assuring the safety, efficacy and security of human and veterinary drugs, biological products, medical devices, our nation's food supply, cosmetics, and products that emit radiation.[26]

---

[25] 1984 Wendy's hamburger chain advertisement theme and catchphrase.

[26] "What We Do." U.S. Food and Drug Administration: What We Do. www.fda.gov/AboutFDA/WhatWeDo/ (accessed September 14, 2015).

The Financial Accounting and Standards Board (FASB), alternately, looking to CONTROL the accuracy and balance in industry and institutional financial reporting, states:

> The mission of the FASB is to establish and improve standards of financial accounting and reporting that foster financial reporting by nongovernmental entities that provides decision-useful information to investors and other users of financial reports.[27]

NATO as a multinational alliance has a far more expansive vision of STRATEGY:

> *NATO's essential purpose is to safeguard the freedom and security of its members through political and military means.*
>
> POLITICAL—*NATO promotes democratic values and encourages consultation and cooperation on defence and security issues to build trust and, in the long run, prevent conflict.*
>
> MILITARY—*NATO is committed to the peaceful resolution of disputes. If diplomatic efforts fail, it has the military capacity needed to undertake crisis-management operations. These are carried out under Article 5 of the Washington Treaty—NATO's founding treaty—or under a UN mandate, alone or in cooperation with other countries and international organizations.*[28]

The point to take in is that regulatory bodies perforce, migrate, and cluster their major efforts around one or more of the Institutional Imperatives we have enumerated. Wise lobbyists and governmental relations professionals will take care to analyze the prime concerns of the regulators active in their markets, and shape their regulatory liaison efforts around these Institutional Imperatives.

---

[27] "FASB, Financial Accounting Standards Board." Facts About FASB. www.fasb.org/facts/ (accessed September 14, 2015).

[28] "What Is NATO?" www.nato.int/nato-welcome/index.html (accessed September 14, 2015).

Return to List: Some Parameters through Which Institutional Imperatives Cycle.

Some Diagnostic Approaches to Service Management

Unique Service Climates Relevant to the Five Institutional Imperatives

In each domain of the punctuated spectrum we have been exploring, there are modulations in the profile of any service offering that will govern that offering's success or failure.

To keep our analysis compact, we will approach this schematically, looking to the three basic *vectors* we established early on in the discussions of the section titled Time-Invariant Market Structure: The Commodities & Breakthroughs Spectrum.

They are as follows:

- The *judgmental* vector governing *economics*: *Price*, Cost, Value
- The *volitional* vector governing *possession* and *access*: *Availability*, Delivery, Readiness
- The *intellectual* vector of material *acceptability*: Anticipated *Quality*

The conditions in these parametric *climates* undergo rolling shifts as the executive buyer, the incumbent in each of the Intent-driven Cockpits managing in each of the five domains is driven by his relevant Institutional Imperative.[29]

Going forward through the treatment of the five institutional imperatives driving their incumbent executives, it is important to notice the rolling modulation, those *climates* in the three aforementioned parameters. They start out with a decided commodity flavor, and end up with a market-making breakthrough stance. The stepwise modulation through the five domains is never an algorithmic process, but instead is more a depiction of the art of the possible at each stage.

---

[29] Our now-familiar friends: DELIVERY, *efficiency*, CONTROL, *planning*, STRATEGY.

Going forward now, we examine what transpires generally in each Intent-Driven Cockpit …

At the DELIVERY Level

SYMMETRY IN OPPOSITION: COMMODITIES AT **DELIVERY** LEVEL				
DELIVERY	*efficiency*	CONTROL	*planning*	STRATEGY
▼				
STANDARD QUALITY				
STANDARD PRICE				
SHELF AVAILABILITY				

- PRICE is usually preset, either out of a catalogue, or a sales manual, or a corporate purchasing agreement; anything that materially alters that number is either cause for alarm, or if a discount somehow materializes, for happy escalation to higher management;
- AVAILABILITY is generally a prenegotiated date and quantity so as not to unsettle production systems depending on predictable feeds. If supply of some materiel can ship out early, there will be questions about interim warehousing at the receiving end;
- QUALITY is, again, usually well understood before any discussion is undertaken about contract signing; the quality of the offering has to support the production process into which it is injected, and premium elements of quality may be seen as distractions rather than enhancements.

In this climate, the cocreation of value stands or falls on the cementing of great vendor reliability. The service supplier wins who is seen as an intimate partner with the DELIVERY executive in keeping the production systems humming. Excellence in service in this environment boils down to avoiding unpleasant surprises at all costs and advertising that dependable performance in periodic, pleasant updates to at least the next level above, that of the *efficiency* executives.

When a change in any of the three base parameters is foreseen, whether it is positive or adverse, the vendor of the service should forecast this change to the DELIVERY executive as early as feasible to allow for adjustments and alerts to go up that executive's chain of command, and to allow for returning reconnaissance to reach the vendor in question if there is an adverse reaction to the forecast change in PRICE, AVAILABILITY, or QUALITY.

In sum, whether proposing, implementing, or maintaining, at this level, the leitmotif is "WE DELIVER!"

At the *Efficiency* Level

SYMMETRY IN OPPOSITION: COMPONENTS and SUBSYSTEMS AT *efficiency* LEVEL				
DELIVERY	*efficiency* ▼	CONTROL	*planning*	STRATEGY
STANDARD QUALITY With Featured Component Additions and Some Engineering				Some Elements of Installation Risk
PRICE With some special pricing and inclusion of support services				Some Estimates of Cost Reduction/Avoidance
SHELF AVAILABILITY With some scheduling of upgrade components				Some Enhancement Scheduling Exposure

The three parameters begin to modulate toward a grammatical comparative: "*better*."

In the instance of the *efficiency* executive:

- PRICE begins to show variances on a base cost. Because the vendor is proposing an enhancement to an existing process, there will generally be choices made as to how far any refurbishing or addition of functionality should be taken; the settled PRICE called for at the preceding level begins to be more strongly affected here by shadings of perceived VALUE. A common query at this level is "What's this new feature worth to me and my operation?"
- AVAILABILITY, generally a prenegotiated date and quantity, sees some pressure at this level, because of inventory, installation, or service provider scheduling. It now becomes more palatable to suggest early implementation, in that the acquisition is for something to enhance a base process or subsystem, rather than to install one outright. Warehousing concerns wane markedly;

- QUALITY, as well, begins to show some blurring, in that, part of its impact is projected, a promised aspect of the improved, more efficient enhancement. It takes time to verify that the promised efficiency is happening and flowing to the bottom line.

In this climate, the cocreation of value depends on the acquirer accepting the premise of the vendor's claim to add value by a proposed enhancement to existing processes or subsystems. The promise of "better" has to be accepted and acknowledged in feedback between vendor and user.

The service supplier wins who is a knowledgeable partner of the *efficiency* executive, versed in improving existing operations. Excellence in service in this environment boils down to promising, and delivering "better," that is, increased efficiency and decreased or avoided costs.

In that the vendor at this level is proposing a recurrent journey of incremental change, success at this level requires finesse in proposing only enough change to be digestible and more than enough to make a discernible difference in the bottom line in reduced or avoided costs.

In sum, the leitmotif at this level is: We make it *"better."*

At the CONTROL Level

SYMMETRY IN OPPOSITION: FUNCTIONAL SYSTEMS AT **CONTROL** LEVEL				
DELIVERY	*efficiency*	**CONTROL**	*planning*	STRATEGY
		▼		
PROCESS CONTROL SYSTEMS				
ROI BOOKED AND TRACKED				
PROJECTS MANAGED TO COMPLETION				

The three parameters begin to seek equilibrium, using terms connoting "balance."

In the instance of the CONTROL executive,

- PRICE now cedes its place to COST, and is yoked to REVENUE, to become the *balance* beam of *controllable* VALUE. This is the predominant concern of the CONTROL executive.

- AVAILABILITY generally becomes one of the negotiable parameters that the CONTROL executive arbitrages to keep in place the financial equilibrium he or she is paid to maintain. If availability of a component of a functional system sets the financial plan of the institution at risk, the CONTROL executive will generally move resource (funds, overtime or temp human resources, emergency backup orders, and so on) into play to offset the shortfall.
- QUALITY for the CONTROL executive is increasingly a *service*-related attribute: Does the vendor have working *credibility* with the DELIVERY and *efficiency* levels of management? Are the vendors' claims *bankable*, *dependable*, and *flexible* enough to allow the CONTROL executive to grant participation in major revisions to control systems where the 24/7 viability of the institution may be in play? We are no longer in the terrain of materiel or of hourly worker contributions, but at the level of consultative service professionals.

In this climate, the cocreation of value depends on the acquirer verifying the capacity of the vendor to act as a trusted advisor, as a subject matter consultant, often on retainer. It is at this level that we begin to see the presence of such permanent advisors as independent accounting firms staffed with CPAs. We also see legal firms with a competence in tax, import and export, and EPA law show up. We see this expensive buttressing of the external position of the institution, because the CONTROL level is the first layer at which we see substantial external regulation appear.

The service supplier wins who is a knowledgeable advisory team to the CONTROL executive, versed in maintaining the financial, legal, and regulatory balance implicit in the corporate plan, whether it be for profit or not-for profit. Excellence in service in this environment boils down to acknowledging that the institution at this level begins to interact intensely, peer to peer with other enterprises and institutions. This realm demands the maintenance of a CONTROL-able public stance in its encounters with its peers, whether in cooperation or competition.

In that the vendor at this level is assuming an advisory posture on changes of substantial weight, it becomes of compelling importance that the advisory team be professionally trained in the specialties they bring to the CONTROL community, whether it be finance, law, ecology, site selection, or whatever else is in play at the time. Their leitmotif is, "We can guide you with assurance and balance."

At the *Planning* Level

SYMMETRY IN OPPOSITION: ARCHITECTURES AT *planning* LEVEL				
DELIVERY	*efficiency*	CONTROL	*planning*	STRATEGY
			▼	
Base Systems Remissioned	*Substantial revisions of lines of business*			
Existing Pricing Structures Recalibrated	*Increased Revenue Streams Arising from LOB Realignment*			
Earlier Contract-Committed Deliverables Provisioned, Shipped	*Acceptable Business Risk*			

The three parameters begin to lean much more toward "incremental revenue at manageable risk."

In the instance of the *planning* executive,

- COST now cedes its dominance to *incremental* REVENUE, and a bias toward change is injected into the working vocabulary of the planning professionals. *Planning* changes to reach incremental REVENUE enhancement is the predominant concern of the *planning* executive.
- AVAILABILITY generally becomes one of the major KPIs[30] of any plan for increasing REVENUE that will be offered out of the planning community. Vendors serving this domain will want to ensure that their proposals for launching new functional systems (marketing, service provisioning, maintenance coverage, operational up-time, and so on) will all promote a solid improvement in the AVAILABILITY of the business systems situated in the broader institutional architecture.

---

[30] KPI: Key Performance Indicator.

- QUALITY for the *planning* executive is predominantly a *service*-related attribute: Does the vendor (now the consulting partner) provide the *planning* executive with timely, accurate, comprehensive counsel? Does the vendor team have credibility with the CONTROL and STRATEGY levels of management? Are the vendors' relationships with external stakeholders (regulators, bankers, potential allies) *bankable*, *dependable*, and *flexible* enough to allow the *planning* executive to grant participation in delimiting expansions of existing markets? We continue on at this level in the terrain of teams of consultative service professionals.

In the *planning* domain, the cocreation of value depends on the acquirer and the subject matter consultant cooperating to plan out pathways to increased revenue from existing corporate initiatives. At this level, it is routine that such permanent advisors, typically on retainer, cooperate to ramp up the performance of the institution. At this level, the various stakeholders—employees, stockholders, regulators, business partners, and so on—will generally have formal liaison groups representing their interests. The *planning* executive and her consulting partners will succeed if they engage these groups to pave the way for the revenue enhancement projects on the *planning* team's drawing board.

The service supplier wins who is a knowledgeable advisory team to the *planning* executive, versed in missionizing the financial, legal, and regulatory enhancements proposed for the corporate plan, whether it be for profit or not for profit. Excellence in service in this environment boils down to acknowledging that the institution at this level interacts daily, intensely, peer to peer with other enterprises and institutions. This realm demands the promotion of a *planned* public stance in its encounters with its peers, its stakeholders, and its governmental authorities, whether in cooperation or competition or compliance.

In that the vendor at this level is assuming an advisory posture on changes of substantial weight, it remains of compelling importance that the advisory team be deeply experienced in the specialties they bring to the *planning* community, whether it be finance, law, ecology, site selection, or whatever else is in play at the time. Their leitmotif is, "Together, we can plan the institution's best course to the most lucrative safe harbors."

At the STRATEGY Level

SYMMETRY IN OPPOSITION: ENVIRONMENTS AT **STRATEGY** LEVEL				
DELIVERY	*efficiency*	CONTROL	*planning*	**STRATEGY**
				▼
				CRITICAL MASS FUNCTION
			UNCERTAIN EXPECTATION OF GAIN	
		ESTIMATED FEASIBILITY PROJECTED, TRACKED		

The three parameters now seek "new markets" at acceptable "business risk."

In the instance of the STRATEGY executive,

- Improving REVENUE now cedes its dominance to MARKET OPPORTUNITIES, and a frank search for new markets, as in: When will the new product family launch begin create demand and throw off cash? Change at this level is a constant in the working vocabulary of STRATEGY professionals. STRATEGIC changes to reach NEW REVENUES mark the predominant concern of the STRATEGY executive.[31]

- AVAILABILITY generally stands as one of the major KPIs[32] of any plan for *creating* REVENUE in a new market to be launched out of the STRATEGY community. Vendors serving this domain will want to ensure that their contributions for launching new market initiatives will all promote a solid foundation in the timely AVAILABILITY of the new business environments launched from the broader institutional architecture.

  Because STRATEGY executives are particularly focused on risk-laden new ventures or partnerships, timeline feasibility becomes admixed into the AVAILABILITY mix: When can the new venture create the demand needed to establish its

---

[31] Daniel Burnham, the late 19th-century architect famously said, "Make no little plans, for they have no magic to stir men's blood and probably themselves will not be realized." Cf. Moore, C. 1921. Chapter XXV, "Closing in 1911–1912." In *Daniel H. Burnham, Architect, Planner of Cities*, p. 1921, Volume 2. (Boston: Houghton Mifflin)

[32] KPI: Key Performance Indicator.

foothold in the projected market, and begin to throw off the anticipated revenues. What are the fallbacks if the project falters in its early infancy? How does it get put back on the rails to be an available source of new revenues?

- QUALITY for the STRATEGY executive is now preeminently a *service*-related attribute, with very little actual injection of materiel: Does the vendor (now the consulting partner) provide the STRATEGY executive with timely, comprehensive *counsel* on the competing interests of the various stakeholders (regulators, bankers, potential allies) surrounding efforts to break open new markets? Does the vendor team have credibility with the CONTROL and STRATEGY levels of management? Are the vendors' relationships with external stakeholders *bankable*, *dependable*, and *flexible* enough to give the STRATEGY executive access to these communities? We continue at this level in the terrain of teams of consultative service professionals.

In the STRATEGY domain, the cocreation of value depends on the acquirer and the subject matter consultant cooperating to execute scenarios chosen to break open new markets and new revenue streams. At this level, it is routine that such permanent advisors, typically on retainer, cooperate to reimagine the societal position of the institution. At this level, the various stakeholders—employees, stockholders, regulators, business partners, and so on, will generally have formal liaison groups representing their interests. The STRATEGY executive and his consulting partners will succeed if they engage these groups to pave the way for the new market and new revenue stream initiatives they've chosen to implement.

The service supplier wins who is a trusted advisory partner to the STRATEGY executive, versed in missionizing the financial, legal, and regulatory revisions proposed for the market space in question, whether it be for profit or not for profit. Excellence in service in this environment boils down to acknowledging that the institution at this level interacts daily, intensely, with top-tier enterprises and institutions. This realm demands the promotion of chosen market development scenarios in its encounters with its peers, its stakeholders, and its governmental authorities, whether in cooperation or competition or compliance.

In that the vendor at this level has assumed an advisory posture on changes of market-making weight, it remains of compelling importance that the advisory team be deeply experienced in the specialties they bring to the STRATEGY community, whether it be finance, law, ecology, polity, site selection, or whatever else is in play at the time. Their leitmotif is, "Together, we can make new markets and earn you our valued client, new authority in the larger social and economic arena."

The Safe-Harbor Phases of Market Process Flow

In that there is a general flow from early breakthroughs opening up new markets and creating new demand, down into maturing commodity markets fully engaged in satisfying matured demand, it becomes important to recognize that there are both relatively quiet pools of operation, and more choppy waters of transition in passing from one tectonic zone to the next. If there are tested incumbents managing the DELIVERY, CONTROL, and STRATEGY portfolios from their respective cockpits, these are areas of market operation where authority is recognized and direction is taken; projects undertaken with the sponsorship of tested incumbents in these areas generally have higher prospects of support and success.

Marketing professionals who aim their messaging around authentic values of DELIVERY, CONTROL, and STRATEGY have a much greater chance of success, especially if their marketing collateral shows clearly how those values coincide with corresponding levels of management operations. Sales professionals as well will find it easier to provide initial benefit statements in their sales calls if they identify incumbent prospects clear about their responsibilities as one of the three: DELIVERY, CONTROL, or STRATEGY.

In corresponding fashion, professionals in marketing will prevail best if, when finding executives operating in the *efficiency* or *planning* levels, they tune their proposals and their marketing collateral to support either of those *missions*. Projects in each of those two layers of management concern are more ephemeral, more vulnerable to being scrapped, and far more varied:

efficiency: "Well, we could bring in and retrain the existing temp workers and upgrade them for the new shift, or we could buy the critical subassemblies from the fab shop we've been using for overflow; or we could just source all the new supply from India."

planning: "I want to know we have a Plan A, Plan B, and a Plan C, with indicators as to how to choose between their scenarios."

Part of the reason for their vulnerability to management rethinking is that they partake of the nature of services far more than the output of the more static three zones. Proposals for increased efficiency, proposals for new plans, both kinds of exercise are information- and performance-intensive, residing largely in white papers, PowerPoint slides, and live briefings. Only after they receive an approving stamp of buy-in, a prime example of executive cocreation of value, do they have better odds of escaping the mercies of the shredder or the off-site storage facility.

Embedded Intelligence: Catalyzing Service into the Dominant Parameter of Value

The whole course of progress in provisioning goods and services has been bound up with its being an increasingly orderly process; one infused with an alert appreciation of the intent held by the potential customer in accepting that offering.

An exemplar of this principle, idealized over time in Hollywood Westerns, is that of the small general store shopkeeper, who knew instinctively the likely needs of his small network of clients as they stepped in through his doors. His service and his product inventory were based on information gained from hourly interaction with his market, constrained only by mercantile deliveries from some larger town to the east. Even those who found his service lacking could upbraid him face to face. His service setting[33] was unconsciously perfect, with frontstage, backstage, and props all

---

[33] Fisk, R., S. Grove, and J. John. 2014. "Chapter 2, Frameworks for Managing the Customer's Experience." In *Service Marketing, an Interactive Approach*, 27. (Mason, OH: SOUTH-WESTERN Cengage Learning).

optimized over time to engage the clients he knew from daily encounter. His information systems were literally his customers.

Alternatively, I remember having boarded a regional[34] Chinese jet in 1994, when the flight attendants, all of them disconsolate young people, began tossing cellophane bags of our presumed in-flight meal at us from more than a few rows away. The flight attendants were so visibly disgruntled that the experience could only be viewed as comedic, had ground crew not been unnerving us all by slamming the landing gear below with sledges.

When my travel companions and I opened our cellophane treasures, we found ominous substances awaiting our further unpacking. There was an aging, desiccated sandwich, ancient fruit sections, and a vague gel in its little tub, accompanied by a general miasmic plume arising from the opened bag. Our intent had been to enjoy, or at least profit from an in-flight repast; it immediately switched to that of Spartan self-denial and gallows humor.

A quick caucus among ourselves revealed complete unanimity; the flight attendants did not care what our expectations or our experience was, unless it led to irreversible comas for each of us.

There was no service setting other than the cabin space through which the cellophane bags sailed; the props were well past their use-by dates and deep into their fumigate-by deadlines. The frontstage of customer service was dirty, and there was no effort to mask off the squabbling that ensured in the backstage galley space once the plane took off.

While that crew was aboard a TU-154, something of a Russian alternative to a Boeing 727, and had the technologies needed to move us from Beijing to Xian, there was a feel about the experience of being trapped inside an airless Industrial Era workhouse: all grudging process, no room for human response. Had there been a heartfelt customer insight offered to that crew, it would have gone unnoticed.

To contrast that experience with the stellar service environment we had on JAL and Singapore Airlines and with the silky professionalism aboard Qantas in the same period, would be cruelty in the service of low humor, and of little value to the modern crop of PRC airline operators.

---

[34] China Northwest Airlines, since merged into China Eastern Airlines.

The point of those recollections is to note an interesting arc in the development of service offerings in the longer history of the market, encapsulated in this graphic:

HISTORIC ARC OF SUPPLY VS MARKET INFORMATION			
HISTORICAL PERIOD	SUPPLY CONSTRAINTS PROBLEMATIC?	MARKET INFORMATION PROBLEMATIC?	SERVICE QUALITY POSSIBLE
PRE-INDUSTRIAL:	Yes	No	EXCELLENT
INDUSTRIAL:	No	Yes	Mediocre
POST-INDUSTRIAL:	No	No	**GOOD** and *IMPROVING*

In the pre–Industrial period, the village shopkeeper was constrained by supply of goods, but quite unconstrained in encompassing in his lived experience, the many wants and needs of his entire small town marketplace.

In the Industrial era, the explosion of manufacturing power allowed floods of goods to reach the market, but with marketer and consumer having to make out of the poorly perceived new availability what they could. As a well-known instance, custom boots went by the boards, and for a while, shoes were mass-produced without the niceties of right- and left-footedness.[35] Information about the individual was disregarded in favor of large-scale data about "the masses."

In our own era, information becomes the coin of the realm, suturing together great precision about our vast sources of supply with that of information about customer buying intent—ideally before that intent becomes consciously noted by the individual consumer.

The lesson for us in our treatment of the Sensorium and its implications for market operations is that the more information we can legitimately glean about the five Institutional Imperatives at play in the enterprises we serve, the more we can approach the idealized marriage of small shopkeeper customer awareness, coupled with the immense provisioning power of our processes of service and product delivery.

---

[35] Frommer, D.W. "A History of the Western Boot." Shoe Infonet. http://shoe-infonet.com/shoe-history/history-western-boot (accessed September 29, 2015).

Determining Whether Your Service Offerings Are Vulnerable to the Discontinuities in the Sensorium

Service offerings are most effective if their definition and their staging are completely congruent with the organizational agendas driving their prospective client. It becomes important to understand where major phase transitions occur within the markets stamped with the architecture of our human sensorium.

If we are architecting an offering, it will serve us best if we ensure that both messaging and actual delivery first align themselves along one of the Institutional Imperatives we've described earlier.

The main body of new offerings, whether service- or materiel-intensive, tends to resonate in the lower reaches of the punctuated spectrum, down at DELIVERY and *efficiency*. This arises because the higher one goes in the spectrum, the more personalized and ephemeral the offering tends to be. This also drives pricing close to the commodity level, rather than to the breakthrough level, where margins can be very high, and engagements can be extended, despite the ephemeral nature of the value add being provided on a given day.

Accordingly, using the two lowest levels in the spectrum, we can pose some simple questions that will indicate the process of vetting one's marketing and one's delivery of services:

1. Is the broader population of one's likely prospects, managers engaged in DELIVERY of an end product? If so, then any marketing message that misses reassurances on dependable delivery of services rendered is an unforced error.

2. If one is dealing with the DELIVERY layer, and does not have in place a visible, robust support environment to ensure the service delivery promised in 1, that is, again an unforced error, a self-inflicted wound.

3. Is the broader population of one's likely prospects, managers engaged in *efficiency* in the production of an endpoint service? If so, then any marketing message that misses reassurances on the enhancement of efficiency one's offering provides in the delivery of services rendered is an unforced error.

4. If one is dealing with the *efficiency* layer, and does not have in place a visible, robust support environment to ensure the service delivery promised in 3, that is again an unforced error, a self-inflicted wound.

The general point can be extended across all five nodes: Lead with both promises and execution, down the precise axis of the Institutional Imperative most in evidence with your main patron.

CHAPTER 5

Interim Conclusions

We have in this volume worked to illuminate the invariant structures: tectonic zones and their interfacial boundaries that our human sensorium imposes on our view of the wider world, especially as we lift our gaze beyond individual contact, out to our larger social structures.

We have worked to illuminate, in particular, the effect these grand patterns impose on our exchanges, and on all our markets.

It falls now to remark about the role of *invariant* Structures and the two other grand strands that make up our view of the world, as apprehended through our sensorium: Processes and Materiel.

A good way to think of this is to visualize a typical internal combustion engine (ICE). The engine block and its mountings is a good example of structure. It is invariant for the life of the engine, saving only radical modifications by teenagers and other speed merchants with large budgets.

The engine block houses various channels and vessels wherein feedstocks may be brought in, admixed, vaporized, detonated, and expelled. Those channels all operate under *temporal* clocking cams, gear ratios, and nowadays, computerized monitor and governors. That complexity all melds together to constitute the various Processes that the ICE Structure supports to generate power.

Finally, there are the feedstocks: lubricating oil, electrical power, gasoline, coolant, and air. These all are metered in by their regulating Processes, maintained in position by the engine block and its ancillary assemblies, to create the motive power the ICE exists to produce.

In a similar fashion, market and exchange architectures can be analyzed in that tripartite fashion. Accordingly, we will now leave for a bit, the world of Invariant Structures; we will proceed to develop an understanding of the companion resources: Process in Volume II, and Materiel in Volume III. As in Volume I, we will relate this all to the

Exchanges and Markets we humans begin evolving as soon as we leave the family for larger social groupings.

The author hopes the current volume has left the reader in command of an understanding of the punctuated vista our human sensorium provides us, and trusts that the reader is prepared to be pleasantly surprised at its reemergence in those two upcoming treatments.

APPENDIX A

The Sensorium Cascades into Markets[1]

Foveal perception	*Saccadic tuning*	Ganglial reduction/ summation	*Saccadic tuning*	Peripheral perception

▼ Vision Coupled with Hearing at the Sensory System Level ▼

Tilting, Nodding Calibration	*Cerebral tuning*	Auditory Perception	*Cerebral tuning*	Tilting, Nodding Calibration

▼ Creates Unified Sensory Perception ▼

Observed Data Points	*Inter-organic tuning*	Inter-Channel Synthesis	*Inter-organic tuning*	Gestalt Perspective

▼ And Supports Tripartite Human Mentation ▼

Facts, INTELLECT	*Discretionary tuning*	Assessments, JUDGMENT	*Discretionary tuning*	Intents, VOLITION

▼ Which Carries Over into Social Interchange ▼

Pooled Information	*Social consensus*	Group Opinion	*Movement in mores*	Societal Norms

▼ And Shapes Institutional Imperatives ▼

DELIVERY	*Efficiency*	CONTROL	*Planning*	STRATEGY

▼ At Macro-Market Levels ▼

TECHNOLOGY *Commodities*	ECONOMICS *Control Systems*	POLITY *Market Formation*

---

[1] We use "mentation" in this *Cascade Chart* because that term more generally describes mental activity; this allows us to distinguish within it the more specific, separate powers of *intellect*, *judgment*, and *volition*.

APPENDIX B

The Roots of Market Structure in Biology and Sociobiology

The Key to Markets: Exchanges

Accepting the basics of our biology, and the growing insights offered by sociobiology, this book builds on the basic insight that **exchanges** are the indispensable engines driving all transactions of value to living beings.

They are at base, transactions that, repeated, introduce complexity and aspects of systematic operation into an entropic environment. Thus far, they are seen to originate from living or "near-living" creatures. An interesting corollary is that they **reduce** the amount of chaos or total information in the environment wherein they are found. That reduction of total information allows for the rise of repeatability, persistence, and living presence at even the most primitive level.

In an ancient instance important to us all, genetic **exchanges** between early precursors of mitochondria and proteobacteria likely started out as accidents.

But in time these exchanges stabilized, recasting the mitochondrial ancestors into subsumed organelles—living power-plants permanently niched within their hosts' cells. This first gave rise to eukaryotic organisms, among which all humans are included.

In like manner, every species works at exploiting multiple exchanges of materiel, to create the elements of a tailored eco-niche supporting the transactions of value to life. Over time, those exchanges will see their **materiel flows** solidify into **optimized processes**; and then **persistent structure** will encrust around those processes to create a durable **architecture** of **exchange**, a nascent proto-market.

Exchanges will always occasion the transfer of assets carrying survival value among the parties to the transaction. One side always sees a gain, at least for a time—the other may not.

Pathogen + Host = Early Collapse of Pseudo-Symbiosis

Pathogens transfer infection into host cells, and host cells provide a viable niche to the pathogen; the pathogen benefits so long as the hosts survive, or new hosts can be found. The host cells may die in their millions until the niche they provide falters; the pathogen then either mutates to provide reciprocal value to the host, jumps species, or itself burns out.

Symbionts + Too-Fragile Niche = Collapse of Symbiosis

Longer-lived exchanges benefit both parties, so long as their supporting niche escapes destruction. Hunnic and Mongol horses and riders raiding as symbiont cavalry, flourished so long as there were vulnerable European cultures to despoil. When they repeatedly depleted those niches, each successive invasion ebbed, their once-fierce forces faltering back toward Asia's Eastern Steppe as relatively harmless herdsmen.

Symbionts + Replenished Niche = Ongoing Fecundity

Truly successful exchanges prosper both transacting parties, and as well, enrich their niches. Plains bison and their preying grey wolf companions kept each other in elegant ecological balance, so greatly enriching the stabilizing Tall Grass Prairie, that the lush, underlying loess soil lay in some locales over three hundred feet deep.

The exchanges of materiel may mediate:

- The physical (food, water, aeration, refuse);
- The topographic (cleared defense arenas, fortified defiles, pathways to resources);
- The informational (neurotransmission between adjacent cells, RNA transcription, and so on);

- The social (dominant versus subordinated roles, nurturing versus aggressive psychologies) or any of a number of other parameters important for species survival; and
- The institutional (currencies, lines of credit, trade pacts, commodities, and so on).

Each of these exchange niches is something of a semiplastic medium, out onto which the strengths and the limitations of the species are projected. This projection carves out of the medium, features of value to the species' survival—and, as well, confronts resistances that limit the species to the boundaries it can defend; the sea shapes sharks, as the air does hawks. These features, pliant or resistant, may be inert materiel, or in the case of symbionts, one or more partnering or subjugated species.

Them

Termite castles in Australia and Africa, structures upwards of twenty feet tall, reflect with great elegance this structural engineering of appropriate niches. These one-centimeter eusocial[1] insects evolved their castle designs over millennia, to house processes and materiel for shelter, aeration, defense, foraging, and the farming of fungal symbionts.[2]

Generally blind, termites cannot live long outside a castle, deprived of its architecture of supporting exchanges. If they swarm, led by their sighted queens and kings, it is to set up a new castle, a new supporting niche with its exchanges replicating the castle from which they emigrated.

Prairie dog towns serve equally well the needs of those highly mobile social mammals constantly under threat of predation by coyotes, bobcats, and various raptor birds. Their towns always include sentinel mounds for on-duty sentries scanning for danger. As well, they provide multiple

---

[1] Cf. *Merriam-Webster*. www.merriam-webster.com/dictionary/eusocial, "Eusocial: living in a cooperative group in which usually one female and several males are reproductively active and the nonbreeding individuals care for the young or protect and provide for the group <eusocial termites, ants, and naked mole rats>" (accessed April 18, 2015).

[2] Termites themselves are symbiont niches for the gut bacteria they host, allowing for the breakdown of cellulose.

entrances and exits for emergency flight, launched when there is invasion by badgers and ferrets. There are also storage areas, food dispersal chambers, and nurseries for pups, reminiscent of the egg hatcheries in termite mounds. All this structure again supports exchange processes vital to the existence of the town's inhabitants.

Us

If those species create exchanges to somewhat shape the outside world to their unique limits and strengths, just so do our human exchanges evidence our own tailoring impulse.

The Hellenic temple of Apollo at Delphi had the inscription "Know Yourself"[3] engraved prominently in its forecourt. In the instance of our topic of grasping the structures of markets, it can perhaps be extended: Know yourselves, to understand your exchanges and your markets.

Accordingly, this book treats our markets as exchanges evolved to meet needs unique to humans. They reflect our deep prehistory as Homo sapiens, engaged as we've been in their operations over millennia. It will also highlight the unique features "humanizing" for our species the major elements found across all exchange architectures: **Structure; Process; Materiel**.

These features of our markets will be explored as projections from within us up into the abstract spaces of technology, economics, and polity. These spaces will have on them our own stamp as social beings solving anew the evolutionary puzzle of cooperation and competition shown us by the work of Konrad Lorenz, E.O. Wilson,[4] and others.

If who and what we are shapes how our earliest exchanges evolved into markets, it becomes important to piece out what in our makeup governs most, the configurations our exchanges—our markets take.

---

[3] γνῶθι σεαυτόν or gnóthi seaftón
[4] Lorenz, K. 1963. *On Aggression*. (Orlando, FL: Harcourt Brace). Print; Wilson, E.O. 1975. *Sociobiology: The New Synthesis*. (Cambridge, MA: Belknap Press of Harvard University Press). Print; Wilson, E.O. 2012. *The Social Conquest of Earth*. 1st ed. (New York: Liveright Pub).

Doin' What Comes Naturally

Think Again

It is by now long a truism that *Homo sapiens* has sustained an explosive expansion of the cerebrum, and a consequent recalibration of the complementing structures in our brain. This remains our nature's most distinguishing characteristic, and one that governs all the other changes shaping our development from earlier hominins. But that great increase in mental capacity has not arisen in a vacuum. Other changes have cooperated to give that capacity its extraordinary reach and range. We must look elsewhere for these further, distinguishing characteristics.

Not All Thumbs

It's easy to raise bipedalism, prehensile thumbs, and binocular vision as elements that make us particularly human, until we look at the cousins in the family, chimpanzees and bonobos. There they are with their own bipedalism and prehensile thumbs, staring back at us with their own binocular vision.

If we raise the more abstract features, tool making and use, we know that New Caledonian crows modify and use twigs as ant and grub gathering tools, and even to explore unfamiliar objects.[5] And we know now that Senegalese chimpanzees shape small branches into ad hoc spears for hunting,[6] and that dolphins collect and use sponges while foraging to buffer themselves against abrasive seafloors.[7] So to what do we look for our unique stamp on the exchanges in our niche?

---

[5] Wimpenny, J., A. Weir, and A. Kacelnik. December 24, 2010. "New Caledonian Crows Use Tools for Non-Foraging Activities." *Animal Cognition*. http://link.springer.com/journal/10071 (accessed April 12, 2015).

[6] Yirka, B. April 15, 2015. "Chimps in Senegal Found to Fashion Spears for Hunting." http://phys.org/news/2015-04-chimps-senegal-fashion-spears.html (accessed April 15, 2015).

[7] "Mystery of Dolphin Tool Use Solved by GU Researchers." Georgetown University. July 20, 2011. http://phys.org/news/2012-07-dolphins-sponge-culture.html (accessed April 09, 2015).

Human Sensory Channels (Our Unique Sensorium) Determine Structure in Proto-Markets

It's a Sensation!

Human senses are the channels through which we map the world into our minds, to drive **knowledge**, **judgment**, and **volition**. Coevolving with our greatly expanded cerebral cortex, our senses help dictate our own very species-unique plusses and minuses.

We do not have the surreally effective fighter pilots' eyes of dragonflies or the simple eyespots of starfish, registering mainly, moving gradients of light and dark. We do have eyes that saw one of us safely across thirty-three solitary hours of North Atlantic navigation to land at Le Bourget in 1927.

Our ears hear a range effective for our ancestors' challenges, but fall deaf against those of nocturnal predators like bats and owls. Yet again, we do have ears that have tuned the composition of *Firebird Suite*, the mysterious expanses of silence in the works of Olivier Messiaen,[8] and the very particular Gunnery Sergeant's growl of a Harley-Davidson *Iron 883*.

What then will we learn of our markets when we inspect our own repertoire of senses? First, we set aside the senses conjoined with more ancient elements of the human brain, as in the somatosensory cortex and its pathways out to the body's peripheries. These senses operate at the lower edge of conscious awareness, keeping us in somatic and spatiotemporal balance.[9] All animal species have some form of these; ours are not salient factors in our exchanges and markets.

We look instead to those senses particularly involved in conscious activity, to find the unique human flavor they impart to our own niches.

---

[8] Messiaen is likely the sole person who could completely appreciate his work; he was a chromesthesiac, seeing distinctive colors associated with the various notes and tones in his music.

[9] For example, Protopathic and epicritic sensibilities, exteroception, interoception, proprioception, and so on. Cf. Nolte, J. 2002. *The Human Brain*. 5th ed. Missouri: Mosley. Among humans who are indeed in conscious touch with these senses are competition athletes. Marathoners in only one race will "hear and feel" more oddities in their gut and their limbs than others will in a lifetime.

The Eye of the Beholder

So to begin, where do we look? That very act of *looking* betrays the path; we start with human sight. Or rather with our separate, sidelong systems of sight: foveal and peripheral vision.

These channel systems evidence roughly the kind of allocation of resources relied upon much later, in the development of the communications technology of the 20th and 21st centuries, a spectrum we all refer to today as hardware, firmware, or software.

- Hardware is that invariant mechanical or physical structure supporting computing or communication; hardware doesn't learn; it either works or falls obsolete;
- Firmware is the more flexible process logic that can evolve more quickly than hardware, mediating and summarizing the hard signaling captured by the hardware; and
- Software is the highly variable process logic that can react on the instant to environmental challenges.

Let's start with the "hardware":

- Our foveal system is almost completely composed of perhaps 6.5 million densely packed receptor cones allowing for extremely fine, point-to-point polychrome vision; it covers only 1 percent of our retinal area, but feeds fully 50 percent of our entire visual cortex;

    Our foveal vision finds constant application in instances like the detailed inspection of a path element in an oscillator schematic, undertaken by an electrical engineer, or the close-in study of an uncut diamond through a jeweler's triplet loupe; it resonates best with our acquisition of discrete facts— **knowledge**;
- Our largely color-blind peripheral system, using upwards of 120 million receptor rods, allows for our capture of high-speed motion across a wide, vibratory expanse, responding to the constant jitter of our subconscious, saccadic eye movements.

In turn, our peripheral vision finds constant application, as in the instance of an NFL quarterback using the gestalt sense of his broad field of play to fire off a breakthrough play just as he's plowed under by opposing linemen; this facility resonates with the support of our **volition** and decisions taken against a broad, scintillating tapestry of inputs.

Reducing and summing the output of these two differing physiological systems of sight into an approximation of unified perception benefits from some preprocessing by the minor transition zone between foveal and peripheral structures (the parafovea). But it is in the main, processed by the 1.5 million summarizing retinal ganglion cells.[10]

Their task of summation, however, doesn't itself create for us a smooth panoramic field of view; the motion detection innate in peripheral vision incessantly jitters our foveal vision from one object to another to create that view. Thus, a kind of pixelated spectrum forms in our visual cortex (and unavoidably in our thought); incessantly jumping us between intensely inspected snapshots of objects, and broad-field appreciation of active landscapes.

From this unique human visual apparatus, we get two strong poles of a fundamental framework of human perception, anchoring our specific (foveal) and our general (peripheral) perspectives that so deeply permeate our thinking; we will return to these disparate forms of vision repeatedly, going forward.

Our vision systems can be summarily depicted across this spectrum:

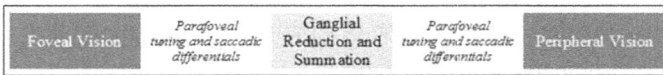

Foveal Vision	Parafoveal tuning and saccadic differentials	Ganglial Reduction and Summation	Parafoveal tuning and saccadic differentials	Peripheral Vision

This yoked-together visual spectrum is weakest in the median, where neither pole of vision is primary, dependent as it is on the reductive summation carried out by the ganglia feeding the visual cortex.

Another sensory system must come in to supplement vision.

---

[10] Hecht, E. 1987. *Optics*. 2nd ed., section. 5.7. (Reading, MA: Addison-Wesley).

I Hear What You're Saying

Over the lifespan of Homo sapiens, hearing has emerged as that supplemental, intermediating sense.

Hearing has a structure that is a bit analogous to that of vision, in that our twinned monaural hearing channels team up to create our binaural hearing. This works best when we're listening head-on, using the neural circuitry of our auditory cortex.

It can calculate the differing times a sound will strike our two ears; and it can do this pretty well in the vertical and horizontal planes, as well as distinguish a bit, the distance of a static source or one that is moving.

Difficulties arise when two equidistant sounds offer identical signals to one ear, creating ambiguity in the neural processing; it then falls to an analogue to our saccadic eye movements to break those ambiguities.

Say What? Well Cock Your Head This Way

Moving our head slightly or cupping our ear with a hand can introduce enough disparity between incoming signals for our auditory circuits to dispel the ambiguity and establish where the sound originates. Thus, we get a spectrum reminiscent of that of vision, but elegantly supplemental to it:

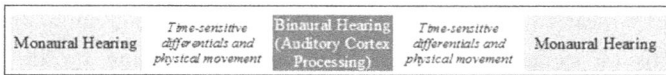

Monaural Hearing	Time-sensitive differentials and physical movement	Binaural Hearing (Auditory Cortex Processing)	Time-sensitive differentials and physical movement	Monaural Hearing

The Human Auditory Spectrum

Now Hear This!

Our reliance on hearing shows up especially wherever there is need for capturing nuance, and particularly for developing group and societal consensus:

> **Social**: "His name is written in Arabic; can you pronounce it for me?"
> **Commerce**: "I saw the slides in your pitch—now let me hear you talk it up and sell it to me."

Military: "Henhouse-Fox to Chicken-Little-2; y'all hearin' what I think I'm hearin'?"

Legislation: "We need a full hearing on your bill; our recaps of it all contradicted each other."

Arts: "Your audition is tomorrow at 10:00 a.m.; with a major Royal Opera figure listening in."

Scholarship: "For your PhD thesis orals; the senior accrediting staff will hear you out."

Justice: "That judge will preside, with a jury of your peers hearing the evidence."

The other of the classic five senses (touch, smell, taste) by now play supporting roles (except in activities like those of masseurs, sculptors, and designers of textured fabrics; chefs, gourmets, and flavorists; perfumiers, florists—and makers of aggressively pungent cheeses—we will not even mention cod-based lutefisk).

Let us now take this comprehensive auditory resource, and see it deployed in the uniquely social interactions that so distinguish Homo sapiens, that of social discourse.

Let's Check Signals

Eusocial and social beings all evidence the need to "compare notes." Our termites appear to use grooming for close proximity signaling, and for more distant signals, pheromones. Termites signal using a wide pheromonal vocabulary, for example, "sex, aggregation, dispersal, alarm, recruitment or trail following, territorial or home range, service or job description, funeral and invitation."[11]

Our prairie dogs use grooming and barking in analogous fashion. But neither our termites nor our prairie dogs evidence anything like the individual intellectual power we each deploy. Our vocal signaling to "compare notes," coevolving with our cerebrum, has hypermorphosed into the unprecedented phenomenon of human hearing and speech.

---

[11] Friend, T. 2004. *Animal Talk: Breaking the Codes of Animal Language*, 121. (New York: Free Press).

This complex function is supported by the rise of specialized cerebral structures: Wernicke's area largely associated with the technically phrased "Receptive Speech" (hearing), and Broca's area largely with its complement, again technically phrased "Expressive Speech."

These capacities, hearing and speech, have evolved as inextricably, "tidally locked" into each other to support our socially directed signaling and comprehension; they are so interwoven that, technically, we might present them coupled together as *Receptive Speech|Expressive Speech*.

Because hearing is the resource Expressive Speech targets, and within which it finds its role, we will instead adopt the vernacular usage of "**hearing**" as the intermediate channel coupling together foveal and peripheral vision. This blended resource allows for the development of **judgment** in the group and societal realms within which human exchanges of all sorts play, as in our aforementioned seven informal examples. As will be seen going forward, hearing-based judgment emerges in a particularly strong role of **control** in our markets.

Having laid in **hearing** as a channel, we now have enough of a breadcrumb trail to offer in progression a view of unified perception at these increasingly complex levels:

- Our sensory systems;
- Our conscious mental activity;
- Social groups within which we interact; and
- The institution, where B2C[12] and B2B markets most clearly emerge.

The Aggregated, Blended Spectrum of Sensory Channels

The aural spectrum we have explored interplays with the two modes of sight to provide more of a continuous spectrum of experience. The interplay of foveal and peripheral vision with hearing creates the three major channels through which we social beings apprehend and understand the realities in our lives.

---

[12] B2C: Business to Consumer; B2B: Business to Business.

Foveal Vision ▼	*Parafoveal tuning and saccadic differentials*	Ganglial Reduction and Summation ▼	*Parafoveal tuning and saccadic differentials*	Peripheral Vision ▼
Monaural Auditory Channel	*Time-sensitive differentials and physical movement*	Binaural Hearing (Auditory Cortex Processing) ▼	*Time-sensitive differentials and physical movement*	Monaural Auditory Channel
+ Channels of Vision and Auditory Processing Yield a Workable Blend +				
Foveal Sight	*Interpolation*	Hearing	*Interpolation*	Peripheral Sight

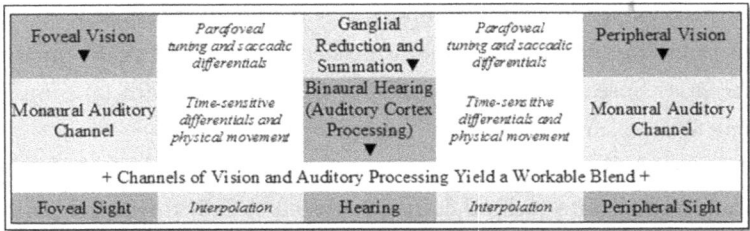

And in Summary …

At this point, it becomes apparent that we are exploring an architecture of sense and intelligence, antecedent to that of market organization. It becomes, for some, unwieldy to encompass the various strands we are interweaving without some consolidation into a graphic. We are providing such in a comprehensive schematic, a bit of an overall roadmap, in Appendix A.

It presents in schematic form this outward flow of traits from our sensory systems into the apperception of our world, as they power a broadening translation of their properties at higher and higher levels of our activity as social beings.

The chart carries the thrust of this book's reliance on the sociobiology underpinning markets to account for their structures, their processes, and their temporal evolutions. It is intended as a continuing reference for the reader inclined to use charts as mnemonics. We are providing it in: Appendix A: The Sensorium Cascades into Markets, so that we may proceed with our analysis.

Going forward, we can reference and use this schema as we work to plot safe courses for our exploration of marketplaces, and for this particular book, those of service offerings in particular. We need now to splice more strands into our matrix.

It's a Triple Play

As noted earlier, we project our internal tripartite segmentation of **intellect**, **judgment**, and **volition** upward into all the group and social arenas within which our intellectual activities, our enterprises, and institutions operate.

These arenas envelop all our intended social interactions; they are the context within which we work out a unique human activity: creating complex objects of **intent**; they will persist as long as humans endure as social beings. They are also the giant pillars of every market that ever has existed or ever will. Let us see how this evidences itself.

For Instance

A very few examples of these projections of ours are:

- Religion: modulation of divinity into trinities where there are varying descriptions of roles;[13]
- Philosophy: segmentation of existence into triads: Plato,[14] Aristotle,[15] and so on;
- Popular literature: Arthur C. Clark's *Rendezvous With Rama*[16] introduces aliens who exclusively operate in triplet fashion;
- Strategy Games: Chess with its classic segments: Opening Gambit, Mid-, and End-Games;

---

[13] Buddhism: the three kayas (manifestations) of the Buddha: unitary, blissful, physical, as well as the Three Jewels (the Triratna); Christianity: Yahweh as Creator, Christ as Savior, the Holy Spirit as Advocate; Hinduism: Brahma as Creator, Vishnu as Preserver, Shiva as Destroyer. There are even subdued hints of trinity in Muslim Sufi poetry, specifying Lover, Beloved, and Love itself as three aspects of the single divinity. Cf. Tarji-Band poem of Hatef Esfehani cited in: Nasr, S.H. 1973. *Sufi Essays*, 136. (Albany: State University of New York Press).

[14] In his various texts, Plato examines various clusters of his archetypal ideas, often as triplets: The NeoPlatonists, particularly Plotinus struggled to reduce these to a tripartite canon: the Good, the True and the Beautiful, the One, The Intellect, the Soul. Cf. Gerson, L. June 30, 2003. "Plotinus." Stanford University. http://plato.stanford.edu/entries/plotinus/#2 (accessed April 23, 2015).

[15] Aristotle subdivides all science using the triplet: the Productive, the Practical, and the Theoretical, Cf. Topics, 145a; cf. Metaphysics, 1025b, and Shields, C. September 25, 2008. "Aristotle." Stanford University. http://plato.stanford.edu/entries/aristotle/ (accessed April 23, 2015).

[16] Clarke, A.C. 1973. *Rendezvous with Rama*, 256. (New York: Harcourt Brace Jovanovich).

His book teases us with the concluding line: "The Ramans do everything in threes."

- Folkloric literature: The Welsh and Irish *Triads of the Island of Britain*;[17] *Irish Triads*;[18]
- Societal: the *Three Estates* of *Ancien Régime* France and other European nationalities;
- Government: separation of powers into three branches: legislative, judicial, executive;
- Military Doctrine: segmentation into tactics, operations, and strategy; and
- Business: missions supporting offering **delivery**, financial **control**, and strategic **leadership**;

In those triplet instances segmenting social groups, there persists an intensely debated tension over priority among the three elements. In business, a somewhat static reading of the institutional hierarchy that's most clear and most germane to our purposes is this:

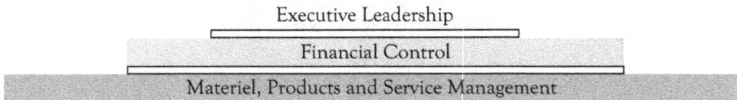

Executive Leadership

Financial Control

Materiel, Products and Service Management

This classic hierarchy of power actually is challenged daily in the arena of executive ambition and power. Endless struggles are waged, as when underinvestment in materiel and service lines drives the technology community in a corporation to stage a putsch, to get more focus on pushing the offerings to the forefront of the market.

This may occasion the appointment of a CEO with a heavy engineering background, with him serving until the question before the corporation is no longer in a crisis of technical relevance in the market.

Similarly, if the finance community sees the financial balance of the institution faltering, a finance personality will often ride to the rescue with a refinancing plan, and serve as either de facto or formal CEO until financial rigor is reasserted.

---

[17] Bromwich, R. 1961. *Trioedd Ynys Prydein: The Welsh Triads*. (Cardiff: University of Wales Press).

[18] Meyer, K., (ed. and Tr.). 1906. *The Triads of Ireland*. Todd Lecture Series 13. (Dublin: Royal Irish Academy).

A separate treatment can show that there is a natural history in long-lived institutions[19] of fraught but cyclical, rolling handoffs out of one of the three communities over into the next, as the institution confronts the limitations of one or another of the three communities to handle current challenges.

That static view of the hierarchy nonetheless tends to represent a corporation in ideal balance. That tripartite segmentation resonates elegantly with a mapping across our broad categories of materiel, process control, and organizational intent. And it fits tongue and groove with the three major market arenas we've accounted for in the following matrix chart:

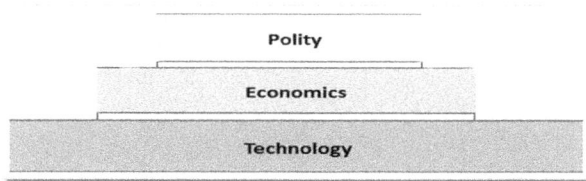

While it does provide that tripartite base, this resultant spectrum does have apparent lacunae interspersed between the three main nodes. And business and markets do not operate well with such discontinuities.

As in the instance of human senses, where ancillary senses and cellular summation "fill in the blanks" to tune the gaps among foveal vision, hearing, and peripheral vision, so do there exist transition zones between materiel and service management, financial control, and executive leadership.

To help distinguish and define both—the three major focal points of institutional activity and the transition zones—it will later become important to distinguish between FUNCTIONS and *missions*.

We will again take up and develop these issues of FUNCTIONS and *missions* back in the main body of the text as we explore markets more explicitly.

---

[19] A history of the first 80 years of IBM operations vividly shows this to hold—Depression, global war, technology revolutions, notwithstanding. For a graphic on this, please refer to Appendix C: Cycles Between Production, Finance, and Market Strategy at IBM.

For now, we've laid in the biological and sociobiological underpinnings of the architecture of the Human Sensorium and its imprint on larger human social constructions.

We accordingly close this Appendix, and suggest rejoining the running text at the breakpoint on Page 12.

APPENDIX C

Cycles Between Production, Finance, and Market Strategy at IBM

AN EVOCATIVE IBM CASE STUDY: CYCLES IN EXECUTIVE AGENDAS

DEMAND CREATION AGENDA DOMINATES
DEMAND SATISFACTION AGENDA DOMINATES
FINANCIAL CONTROL AGENDA DOMINATES

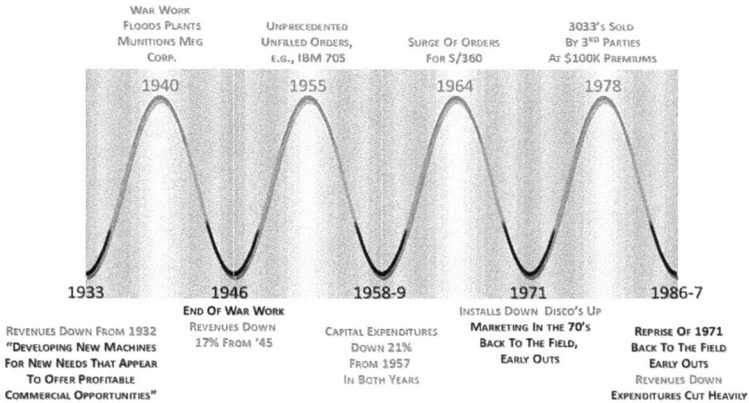

WAR WORK
FLOODS PLANTS
MUNITIONS MFG
CORP.

1940

UNPRECEDENTED
UNFILLED ORDERS,
E.G., IBM 705

1955

SURGE OF ORDERS
FOR S/360

1964

3033's SOLD
BY 3RD PARTIES
AT $100K PREMIUMS

1978

1933

REVENUES DOWN FROM 1932
"DEVELOPING NEW MACHINES
FOR NEW NEEDS THAT APPEAR
TO OFFER PROFITABLE
COMMERCIAL OPPORTUNITIES"

1946
END OF WAR WORK
REVENUES DOWN
17% FROM '45

1958-9
CAPITAL EXPENDITURES
DOWN 21%
FROM 1957
IN BOTH YEARS

1971
INSTALLS DOWN DISCO'S UP
MARKETING IN THE 70'S
BACK TO THE FIELD,
EARLY OUTS

1986-7
REPRISE OF 1971
BACK TO THE FIELD
EARLY OUTS
REVENUES DOWN
EXPENDITURES CUT HEAVILY

APPENDIX D

Glossary, Keywords, and Special Terms

Keywords and key terms	Glossary
Abram Maslow	American psychologist, originator of the indispensable Maslow's Hierarchy of Human Needs.
Binaural Hearing	Ability to integrate aural inputs from two sources, as in human hearing.
Breakthrough	A seemingly sudden, dramatic, and important discovery or development; for our purposes, it generally can be identified by showing evidence of: • Promise of great gain, • Great flexibility on the timing of deliverables, • Great forbearance with the minimal function set needed to declare success.
Commodity	A well-understood primary-level product; such are often raw material or primary agricultural inputs to industrial processes; a commodity is bought and sold in markets already conversant with them as resources; they can generally be identified by its showing evidence of: • A highly constrained price or cost; • Almost no flexibility on the timing of delivery to the client; and • Almost no flexibility on the composition and attributes of the deliverable.

(Continued)

(Continued)

Keywords and key terms		Glossary
Foveal Vision		Acute, detail, colorcapable vision supported by the *fovea centralis* (central pit) in the eye. Humans have a single fovea centralis; American eagles have two: the *deep* fovea and the *shallow* fovea, optimizing the creature for avian predation.[1]
Institutional imperatives	DELIVERY	Management requirement to consistently produce and distribute service or materiel product.
	Efficiency	Management requirement to improve production and distribution of a service or materiel product.
	CONTROL	Management requirement to control and balance production and strategic concerns of an enterprise.
	Planning	Management requirement to offer realistic plans to improve returns from the production and distribution of service or materiel products.
	STRATEGY	Management requirement to seek and exploit opportunities to produce and distribute new service or materiel products in new markets.
Intent-Driven "Cockpit"		The office in each of the five Institutional Imperatives mentioned previously, where the incumbent executive manager plans and programs strictly relevant to the Imperative in question.
Parafovea (Parafoveal Belt)		The transition zone around the fovea centralis providing some continuity between foveal and peripheral vision.
Peripheral Vision		Broad-vista sight, color-blind in nature, which provides supplemental context vision for that of foveal vision.
Punctuated Spectrum		A spectrum with internal zones of different character that create transitional disjuncture.

---

[1] Tucker, V.A. n.d. "The Deep Fovea, Sideways Vision and Spiral Flight Paths in Raptors." *Journal of Experimental Biology*. Web. February 10, 2016. http://jeb. biologists.org/content/203/24/3745.long

Sensorium (pl. sensoria)			The complete complex of human sensory channels; in this work we concentrate not on those serving the solar plexus, but those serving the cerebral faculties of the human.
Value Cocreation			The concept describing the need for both buyer and seller to cooperate on the creation of an acquired good or service, for value transmission actually to occur.
Couplets of Elemental Value:	Commodity	Breakthrough	The couplet highlighting the inverse or oppositional symmetry between commodities and breakthroughs.
	Price	Value	The couplet highlighting the inverse or oppositional symmetry between commodity price and breakthrough value, as yet un-denominated.
	Availability	Feasibility	The couplet highlighting the inverse or oppositional symmetry between the usual finished-goods inventories associated with commodities and the "iffy" nature of delivery of the constituents of still-developing breakthroughs.
	Limited Quality	Critical Mass Function	The couplet highlighting the inverse or oppositional symmetry between the known, delimited value attributes of commodities, and the amorphous, but potentially market-making prospects for value generally found in breakthroughs.

References

"BibleGateway." n.d. Judges 16:21 KJV. N.p. Web. May 12, 2015.

Braudel, F. 1982. *Civilization and Capitalism, 15th–18th Century: The Perspective of the World*. Vol. III. New York: Harper & Row. Print.

Braudel, F. 1981. *Civilization and Capitalism 15th–18th Century. The Structures of Everyday Life: The Limits of the Possible*. Vol. I. N.p.: Harper & Row. Print.

Braudel, F. 1982. *Civilization and Capitalism 15th–18th Century: The Wheels of Commerce*. Vol. II. N.p.: Harper & Row. Print.

Cameron, J. n.d. "'Avatar' Movie Plot Summary." IMDb. N.p. Web. September 28, 2015.

Clarke, A.C. 1973. *Rendezvous with Rama*, 288. New York: Harcourt Brace Jovanovich. Print.

Constantin, J.A., and R.F. Lusch. 1994. *Understanding Resource Management: How to Deploy Your People, Products, and Processes for Maximum Productivity*. Oxford, OH: Planning Forum. Print.

"FASB, Financial Accounting Standards Board." n.d. Facts About FASB. N.p. Web. September 14, 2015.

Fisk, R., S. Grove, and J. John. 2014. "Chapter 2, Frameworks for Managing the Customer's Experience." *Service Marketing, an Interactive Approach*, 27. Mason, OH: South-Western Cengage Learning. Print.

Frommer, D.W. n.d. "A History of the Western Boot." Shoe Infonet. N.p. Web. September 29, 2015.

Gould, S.J. 1999. *Rocks of Ages: Science and Religion in the Fullness of Life*. New York: Ballantine Pub. Group. Print.

Hecht, E. 1987. *Optics*. 2nd ed. N. pag. Reading, MA: Addison-Wesley. Print.

Hyde, L. 2007. *The Gift: Creativity and the Artist in the Modern World*. New York: Vintage. Print.

Kotler, P., and K.L. Keller. 2011. *Marketing Management*. 14th ed. Harlow, UK: Pearson Education.

Lam, B. August 27, 2015. "The Secret Suffering of the Middle Manager." *The Atlantic*. Atlantic Media Company. Web. August 31, 2015.

Lorenz, K. 1963. *On Aggression*. Orlando, FL: Harcourt Brace. Print.

Maslow, A.H. 2013. *Hierarchy of Needs: A Theory of Human Motivation*. N.p.: Martino Fine. Print.

Meyer, R. December 12, 2013. "No Old Maps Actually Say 'Here Be Dragons.'" *The Atlantic*. N.p. Web. April 4, 2015. www.theatlantic.com/technology/archive/2013/12/no-old-maps-actually-say-here-be-dragons/282267/

Miller, J.G. 1978. *Living Systems*. New York: McGraw-Hill. Print.

Misselden, E. 1971. *The Circle of Commerce: Or the Balance of Trade*. Facsimile Edition of 1623 Original ed. New York: A. M. Kelley. Print.

Moore, C. 1921. Chapter XXV, "Closing in 1911–1912." In *Daniel H. Burnham, Architect, Planner of Cities*, p. 1921, Volume 2. Boston, MA: Houghton Mifflin.

"Mystery of Dolphin Tool Use Solved by GU Researchers." July 20, 2011. Georgetown University. N.p. Web. April 9, 2015.

Nasr, S.H. 1973. *Sufi Essays*, 136. Albany, NY: State University of New York. Print.

Nolte, J. 2002. *The Human Brain*. 5th ed. Missouri, MO: Mosley. Print.

"The Secrets of Southwest's Continued Success." 2012. *The Economist*, June 18. N.p. Web. May 6, 2015.

"Selections from Plato's Republic: Book VII, The Allegory of the Cave." n.d. N.p. Web. July 23, 2015. www.anselm.edu/homepage/dbanach/repub7.htm

"Sensorium." *Merriam-Webster*. n.d. N.p. Web. July 20, 2015.

Shakespeare, W. 2005. *Henry VI*. Vol. Part II, Act IV, Line 73, N. pag. New York: Signet Classics. Print.

Shostack, L. n.d. "Frameworks for Managing the Customer's Experience." N.p.: n.p., N. pag. Print.

Singer, K. 1958. Oikonomia: An Inquiry into Beginnings of Economic Thought and Language. S.l.: S.n. Print.

Spohrer, J.C., and L.E. Freund. 2013. *Advances in the Human Side of Service Engineering*. Boca Raton, FL: Taylor & Francis. Print.

"Suit Against Southwestern Bell in 4th Week of Trial." n.d. *The Times-News—Google News Archive Search*. *The Times News*, Hendersonville, NC. Web. September 7, 2015.

"T-Shaped Professionals." n.d. The Service Thinking Framework. CVC Group, Web.

Tucker, V.A. 2000. "The Deep Fovea, Sideways Vision and Spiral Flight Paths in Raptors." *Journal of Experimental Biology* 203, no. 24, pp. 3745–54. Web. February 10, 2016. http://jeb.biologists.org/content/203/24/3745.long

Vargo, S.L., and R.F. Lusch. 2004. "Evolving to a New Dominant Logic for Marketing." *Journal of Marketing* 68, no. 1, pp. 1–17. Web.

Wharton, R. 2012. "Fortune as a Metaphor for the Medieval Church." The Life Death and Afterlife of Geoffrey Chaucer. N.p. Web. August 12, 2015.

"What Is NATO?" n.d. N.p. Web. September 14, 2015.

"What We Do." n.d. US Food & Drug Administration: What We Do. N.p. Web. September 14, 2015.

Wilson, E.O. 2012. *The Social Conquest of Earth*. 1st ed. New York: Liveright Pub. Print.

Wilson, E.O. 1975. *Sociobiology: The New Synthesis*. Cambridge, MA: Belknap of Harvard University Press. Print.

Wimpenny, J., A. Weir, and A. Kacelnik. December 24, 2010. "New Caledonian Crows Use Tools for Non-Foraging Activities." *Animal Cognition*. N.p. Web. April 12, 2015.

Yirka, B. April 15, 2015. "Chimps in Senegal Found to Fashion Spears for Hunting." N.p. Web.

Index

www.ingramcontent.com/pod-product-compliance
Lightning Source LLC
Chambersburg PA
CBHW062042200326
41519CB00017B/5104